The Emotional Curriculum

A Lucky Duck Book

The
Emotional
Curriculum
A Journey Towards Emotional Literacy

Sue Cornwell
Jill Bundy

Los Angeles • London • New Delhi • Singapore • Washington DC

© Sue Cornwell and Jill Bundy 2009

First published 2009

Photographs © Jason Wood 2009
Illustrations by Philippa Drakeford © Philippa Drakeford 2009

SAGE Publications Ltd
1 Oliver's Yard
55 City Road
London EC1Y 1SP

SAGE Publications Inc.
2455 Teller Road
Thousand Oaks, California 91320

SAGE Publications India Pvt Ltd
B 1/I 1 Mohan Cooperative Industrial Area
Mathura Road, Post Bag 7
New Delhi 110 044

SAGE Publications Asia-Pacific Pte Ltd
33 Pekin Street #02-01
Far East Square
Singapore 048763

Library of Congress Control Number 2008933576

British Library Cataloguing in Publication data

A catalogue record for this book is available from the British Library

ISBN 978-1-4129-1237-2 (pbk)

Typeset by C&M Digitals (P) Ltd., Chennai, India
Printed in India by Replika Press, Pvt. Ltd
Printed on paper from sustainable resources

Contents

CD Rom Content

To contents of the Appendicies are printable from the accompanying CD Rom.

1   Happy/Sad Cards
2   Feelings Cards
3   Feelings Chart: How Do I Feel Today?
4   Situation Cards
5   Emotion Cards, Feeling Cards
6   Feelings Diary (Year 2)
7   Feelings Diary (Year 3)
8   Feelings Diary (Year 4)
9   Action Cards
10 Thought Cards
11a Emotional Transitions
11b Emotional Transitions
12a How Do They Feel and How Can You Help? (Sarah)
12b How Do They Feel and How Can You Help? (Phillip)
13 Simultaneous Feelings/Prompt Cards for Role Plays
14a Emotion Cards (words)
14b Emotion Cards (pictures)
15a Action Cards (words)
15b Action Cards (pictures)
16 Role Play Scenarios
17 What is Acceptable and What is Unacceptable
18 Managing My Emotions (1)
19 Managing My Emotions (2)
20 Ambiguous Scenarios/Pictures
21 Role Play Scenarios
22 Personal Profiles
23 Ways of Dealing With Conflict
24 Negotiation

Acknowledgements

Many thanks to our parents for their unceasing encouragement in helping us to finish this book. Our thanks go to Jill's parents and Cyril for proofreading. Our thanks also go to George Robinson and Mel Maines for their support and guidance.

Our thanks go to Molly, Max and Marek for providing us with such expressive faces at very short notice, and to Jason for taking the photographs.

Finally, we wish to thank the many children, and especially Victoria and Emma, whose emotions we have both enjoyed and endured over the years, without whom there would not have been the motivation to write this book.

1

Introduction and Background

Research indicates that emotionally literate people perform better in many areas of their lives. Durlak (1995) and Durlack and Wells (1997) found that programmes teaching social and emotional competencies result in a wide range of educational gains including improved school attendance, higher motivation and higher morale. Greenhalgh (1994) found that learning to manage emotions can assist learning, while Mayer and Salovey (1997) suggest that emotions help us to prioritise, decide, anticipate and plan. In light of these findings there would seem to be a high price to pay for having children who lack the skills associated with emotional competence. Teachers have a key role to play in facilitating the development of those skills that help children to understand and regulate their emotional lives. This will enable children to focus more effectively in school, allowing them to achieve their academic potential.

The Emotional Curriculum has been designed to provide a developmental structure that relates to the key emotional competencies of:

- Recognising and understanding emotions in self (self-awareness).
- Recognising and understanding emotions in others.
- Management and regulation of emotions.
- Relationships.

'Emo' – our feelings friend, whose name is derived from the word 'emotion', is an imaginary creature. The character of Emo is used throughout Key Stage One to deliver some of the material and as a point of reference for younger children. We recommend that you adopt a puppet that you already have in school and name it Emo. This puppet should be used consistently throughout Key Stage One.

The Emotional Curriculum is based on two underlying assumptions: first that the emotional development of children cannot be taken for granted and second that it should be addressed in a proactive manner, through positive teaching and experiences. It was developed following a successful pilot project undertaken in a Bolton primary school. The aim of this project was to determine whether the specific teaching of emotional competencies made a difference to the children's levels of emotional development. We did this, in the first instance, by training the teachers. They were then encouraged to focus their teaching during Circle Time on the basic emotions of happy, sad, angry and afraid. Results demonstrated significant gains in those emotional competencies that were focused on. In particular the children's emotional vocabularies were significantly extended. Children were also able to identify and define their emotions more accurately following a period of specific teaching. The development of these skills resulted in the emergence of a shared language between pupils and between staff and pupils. The head teacher commented that this made behaviour management more intelligent throughout the school. School staff were then keen to have a more structured developmental framework within which to work. We have developed the Emotional Curriculum to meet this need.

Recent government publications such as *Curriculum Guidance for the Foundation Stage* (DfES 2000) encompass the key concepts of social and emotional development. These foundations are then developed throughout the primary and secondary school National Curriculum in subjects such as PSHE, RE and Citizenship. More recent publications such as Weare and Gray (2003) and the Primary National Strategy *Developing Children's Social, Emotional and Behavioural Skills*(DfES 2003), further promote the need for teaching emotional competence within schools. Lastly, *Excellence and Enjoyment: Social and Emotional Aspects of Learning* (DfES 2005) is a resource that should be in every primary school.

What is social and emotional competence?

We have drawn from a broad research base in the development of the Emotional Curriculum. Elias et al. (1997) define social and emotional competence as 'the ability to understand, manage and express the social and emotional aspects of one's life in ways that enable the successful management of life tasks such as learning, forming relationships, solving everyday problems and adapting to the complex demands of growth and development'. The terms emotional intelligence and emotional literacy are also widely used in literature relating to children's emotional development.

Goleman (1995) defined emotional intelligence as 'the ability to understand our emotions and combine them with our rational thoughts, to formulate creative strategies that allow us to achieve our personal best and professional goals'. Goleman also identifies five ingredients to emotional intelligence:

- Self-awareness – knowing one's emotions and recognising feelings as they happen.

- Emotional management – handling feelings, the ability to recover quickly from upsets and distress.

- Self-motivation – the ability to control one's emotions, to self-discipline, delay gratification and stifle impulsiveness in pursuit of one's goals.

- Empathy – the ability to listen and understand what other people are communicating, verbally and non-verbally and to sense what others are feeling.

- Managing emotions in others – the ability to connect inter-personally to others with ease and understanding.

Other prominent researchers in this field include similar competencies or elements in their work. Mayer and Salovey (1997) identify four such competencies:

- The ability to perceive accurately, appraise, and express emotion.

- The ability to access and/or generate feelings when they facilitate thought.

- The ability to understand emotion and emotional knowledge.

- The ability to regulate emotions to promote emotional and intellectual growth.

About the Emotional Curriculum

This curriculum is designed to show the progression of emotional and social competencies throughout the primary years. It contains a list of suggested emotions that can be focused on in each year group. There are four strands of increasing complexity which span the seven year groups:

- Recognising and understanding emotions in self (self-awareness).

- Recognising and understanding emotions in others.

- Management and regulation of emotions.

- Relationships.

The structure of this curriculum is based on the theories of social and emotional competencies outlined in this section. The activities that are described to promote the development of social and emotional competencies take into account a range of learning styles and incorporate various accelerated learning principles. The developmental progression of the curriculum can be seen clearly in the Key Stage One and Key Stage Two tables.

Table outlining the developmental progression of emotional literacy skills across the primary age range: Key Stage One

Year Group		Complexity of emotions	Recognising and understanding emotions in self (self-awareness)	Understanding and recognising emotions in others	Management / regulation of emotions	Relationships
				STRAND		
Nursery/ Reception	School Policy / Ethos promoting Emotional Literacy	Happy, sad	• Ability to remain open to feelings • Ability to recognise own basic emotions	• Ability to recognise basic emotions in others		• Transition from adult-child relationship to playing alongside peers • Developing turn-taking skills
Year 1		+ anger, scared, excited	• Ability to recognise an increased range of emotions in self and talk about own experiences of emotions • Recognise own personal triggers to emotions	• Ability to recognise cues to others' emotions (facial expression/body language)	• Understand the difference between an emotion and an action	• Developing the ability to share • Developing co-operative play skills
Year 2		+ nervous, loved, lonely, bored, worried	• Understanding that all emotions are valid • Recognising cues to emotions	• Ability to recognise others' triggers to emotions and our role in these	• Recognising the range of possible reactions to a variety of emotions and the subsequent need to manage our emotions. • Ability to discriminate between accurate and inaccurate expressions of emotions	• Developing an understanding and appreciation of friendships

Table outlining the developmental progression of emotional literacy skills across the primary age range: Key Stage Two

STRAND

School Policy / Ethos promoting Emotional Literacy

Year Group	Complexity of emotions	Recognising and understanding emotions in self (self-awareness)	Understanding and recognising emotions in others	Management / regulation of emotions	Relationships
Year 3	+ shy, frustrated, relaxed	• Awareness of opportunity to engage with or detach from feelings • Non-verbal expression of emotions	• Ability to engage with or detach from others emotions	• Appropriate ways of dealing with feeling angry, afraid, worried and lonely	• Developing the skills required for successful group work • Recognising individual strengths and weaknesses
Year 4	+ selfish, disappointed, jealous, miserable	• Recognise physiological changes associated with emotions • Recognising that feelings can change and why	• Ability to recognise effects of own mood / behaviour on emotions of others and vice-versa	• Managing a variety of emotional states through the use of relaxation, calming and visual techniques	• Developing an awareness of conflict situations and how these can be resolved
Year 5	+ anger, guilt, shame, pride, embarrassment, grief	• Recognise simultaneous feelings in self • Ability to hide feelings from others	• To develop an awareness of empathy and the ability to demonstrate it • Recognising changes in others' emotions and relating these to events.	• Ability to re-frame situations in a more positive way • Management of grief in self and others	• Developing an understanding of discrimination and equality, focusing on racism and disability
Year 6	Rejection, intimidation, arrogance	• Ability to recognise likely emotional transitions • Taking personal responsibility for own emotions	• Ability to recognise simultaneous feelings in others	• Appropriate ways of dealing with rejection, guilt, jealousy, disappointment and anger • To nurture a desire to use feelings positively	• Developing the skills associated with successful negotiation

2

How to Use the Emotional Curriculum

Aims and objectives of the Emotional Curriculum

The Emotional Curriculum is intended to provide a framework for developing children's social and emotional competence. The framework outlines the expected progression of children's emotional development within the primary years but is not intended to provide a complete scheme of work. The Emotional Curriculum identifies four main strands with specific, age-related objectives for each strand. Exemplars of how these objectives may be achieved are provided. In order to gain the most from this curriculum it is important that you add your own ideas to those suggested. From our experience the teaching of social and emotional competence is most effective when it is given priority throughout a school. When approached in this way we would expect it to have a positive effect on the ethos of the school as well as on individual children's emotional development.

The primary objectives of the Emotional Curriculum are:

- To develop or extend emotional vocabulary.
- To enable pupils to recognise and understand their own emotions.
- To enable pupils to recognise and understand the emotions of others.
- To encourage pupils to express their emotions in appropriate ways through the development of a range of self control strategies.
- To develop the social skills required to establish, develop and maintain reciprocal relationships and friendships.

The character of Emo

The puppet 'Emo' – our feelings friend – is central to the development of social and emotional competencies throughout Key Stage One. You should choose a puppet (this may be one already in school) but the children should not already be familiar with it because this will give you the opportunity to develop Emo's character together. The chosen puppet should be used consistently throughout Key Stage One. The purpose of using a puppet is to deflect strong emotions that children may be feeling, or that you are exploring in class, away from the children and directly onto an imaginary creature. In doing this, children will be able to experience and discuss emotions in a safe context. Many of the activities described in this book relate to Emo.

Circle Time

Circle Time is frequently used throughout this book as a way of meeting identified objectives. It is a regular, structured occasion when a class group meets in a circle to speak, listen, interact and share experiences and concerns. It provides a forum to promote participation and inclusion for all children within the class. Circle Time also provides an opportunity to raise pupils' self-esteem and to promote self-discipline and responsibility towards others. Each Circle Time session is split into three phases, an introductory phase, a middle phase and a closing phase. Each phase has a specific objective. Circle Time is often organised to give every child in the circle the opportunity to speak in turn. An object may be passed around the circle to indicate visually when it is a child's turn to speak, while the rest of the class listen. Techniques such as sentence completion (e.g.-'The last time I felt angry was...') may be useful when encouraging the children to reflect upon and share their own emotional experiences. A non-threatening way to include all children, regardless of their verbal ability, is through the use of silent statements. Silent statements involve someone (usually the teacher) giving a statement accompanied with a non-verbal action (for example, if you have ever been bullied, swap places). This then gives the teacher an indication of children's perceptions or emotions without the child having to verbalise them. For further details and ideas relating to Circle Time please refer to the references at the end of the book.

How to use this book

The remainder of this book explores the strands and objectives outlined in the tables (see p. 4 and p. 5). Each strand begins with an introduction highlighting what the strand contains, why the skills are important, how the skills will help children and examples of how they may be observed. Each objective within the strand is then considered individually and activities suggested. Examples of resources can be found in the appendices.

3

Recognising and Understanding Emotions in Self (Self-awareness)

Introduction

Self-awareness is the ability to recognise, label and communicate to others how you are feeling at any given time. This emotional competence develops from being able to recognise basic emotions such as happiness or sadness to recognising and understanding more complex and subtle emotions such as jealousy, intimidation and grief. Some of the higher order skills associated with the development of self-awareness may be evident in young children. The aim of the Emotional Curriculum is to develop an understanding of these skills, thus giving the children conscious awareness and control over previously unconscious actions. A suggested progression of the competencies involved in developing self-awareness include the ability to:

- o Remain open to feelings.
- o Recognise own basic emotions.
- o Recognise an increased range of emotions in self and talk about own experiences of emotions.
- o Recognise own personal triggers to emotions.
- o Understand that all emotions are valid.
- o Recognise cues to emotions.
- o Be aware of opportunities to engage or detach from feelings depending on their usefulness.
- o Recognise non-verbal expression of emotions.
- o Recognise physiological changes associated with emotions.
- o Recognise that feelings can change and reasons for this.
- o Recognise simultaneous feelings in self.
- o Hide feelings from others.
- o Recognise likely emotional transitions.
- o Take personal responsibility for own emotions.

Each of these competencies will now be considered individually and examples are given of children demonstrating the skill. It is important to remember that because children learn from 'significant others' you as the teacher will be modelling the competencies for the children. Explicit modelling of these skills, including verbally describing what you are doing or have done, will be beneficial for the children.

The ability to remain open to feelings

The ability to remain open to feelings involves children being able to reflect on their feelings on a regular basis, thus acknowledging how they are feeling at any given time. At its most basic this may be a willingness for children to engage in teacher led activities requiring consideration of their emotions.

An example

Children who have developed this skill will be able to cease action in order to think about emotions. Initially this may be in the form of responding to a teacher asking them to think about how they are feeling. Children who are not yet able to remain open to their feelings may demonstrate this through actions such as a refusal to engage.

The ability to recognise own emotions

The ability to recognise one's own emotions involves being able to label and then communicate feelings to another person. The range and complexity of the emotions that children are able to recognise will increase with age and experience. Children who have developed this skill will be able to label an emotion and relate it to themselves. They will also be able to express this emotion to another person.

An example

Abigail arrives in Nursery on her birthday, smiling at the teacher, and tells her that she has been given a baby buggy for her doll. When asked how she feels about this, Abigail is able to respond by saying that she feels happy. In contrast, Rachel, a child who has yet to develop the ability to recognise her own basic emotions may arrive in Nursery on her birthday and report that she has been given a baby buggy for her doll. When asked how she feels about it, Rachel simply re-states that she had got a buggy for the doll. Rachel is not yet able to recognise, label or communicate her feeling to another. In this situation the teacher would need to support Rachel in her development of this skill by suggesting the emotion that she may be feeling. For example the teacher may say to Rachel, 'You look very happy to have a new buggy for your doll Rachel. Do you feel happy?'

The ability to talk about own experiences of emotions

In addition to recognising emotions, children at this stage should be able to talk about times when they have experienced particular emotions. The emphasis is placed on the feeling. Children who have developed this skill will be able to relate feelings to particular events and experiences in their lives and share this knowledge with others.

An example

During a Circle Time session in Year 1, the children were asked to share times when they had felt angry. Matthew responded by saying that he had felt angry when his brother had ripped up one of his paintings. Matthew may also demonstrate this skill when telling the teacher that he feels very sad because his hamster has just died.

The ability to recognise own personal triggers to emotions

The ability to recognise one's own personal triggers to emotions involves an appreciation of a cause-effect relationship. The emphasis is placed on the event that elicits the emotion. Children who have developed this skill will be able to link a preceding event to the way that they are currently feeling.

An example

Richard returns to the classroom after playtime and tells the teacher that he is feeling angry because his friend has been chasing him all playtime. In doing this Richard had clearly identified the relationship between being chased at playtime (trigger) and his feeling of anger.

Recognising that all emotions are valid

Children need to appreciate that all emotions are valid but the way that they are managed is very important. A distinction needs to be made between the emotion and the expression of that emotion. This highlights the link between self-awareness and the regulation of emotions.

An example

The ability to do this can be seen in Paul who appreciates that it is acceptable to feel angry but not acceptable to go around shouting, swearing and hitting people when he feels like this.

The ability to recognise cues to our emotions

The ability to recognise cues to our emotions involves transferring our ability to recognise the emotional cues that we see in others to ourselves. It requires us to make associations between the emotion that we are feeling and how we know we are experiencing that emotion.

An example

During a class discussion focusing on cues to emotions, Jade is able to associate the feeling of excitement with butterflies in her tummy, feeling restless, talking more then usual, wishing for time to speed up and finding it difficult to concentrate on other things. Therefore, she has demonstrated the ability to identify the cues to her emotion.

An awareness of the opportunity to engage or detach from feelings depending on their usefulness

The ability to choose to engage or detach from feelings depending on their usefulness involves an awareness that feelings can be both helpful and unhelpful. This knowledge then needs to be applied in order to make an informed choice.

An example
Julie is producing a piece of writing in class and begins to feel frustrated with her lack of ideas. She recognises that this emotion is not helping her to reach her goal and so she asks the teacher for help. In doing this Julie has recognised the need to try and detach from the unhelpful feeling of frustration.

The non-verbal expression of emotions
An awareness of body language, facial expression and tone of voice is necessary to develop an understanding of how you express your emotions in a non-verbal manner. Children need to be aware of the message that they are giving to others in addition to their spoken language. Teachers have a vital role to play in developing this awareness, thus ensuring that the non-verbal messages being given are consistent with the verbal message.

An example
When apologising to his friend for being unkind, Robert initially said 'sorry' in a sarcastic tone of voice, while scowling with his arms folded. Following teacher intervention, Robert was able to apply his knowledge of non-verbal expression and offer a further apology using a more sincere tone of voice, a more relaxed, open body posture and offered to shake hands.

To recognise the physiological changes associated with emotions
The ability to recognise the physiological changes associated with emotions involves understanding that the body responds in a physical way to emotions and produces a physical response. It requires children to be aware of what their body is telling them. This is one step in enabling children to manage their emotions more appropriately. This is especially important when considering the management of emotions such as anger.

An example
Pat was watching a television programme and her sister kept changing the channel. Pat noticed that she had started to breathe faster and that her palms were becoming sweaty. She recognised these as a sign of increasing anger. She decided to record the programme that she wanted to watch and go and read a book instead. Pat's ability to recognise the physiological changes within her body prevented her from losing her temper.

Recognising that feelings can change and reasons for this
Recognising that feelings can change involves identifying and labelling the emotions experienced. It also requires an understanding of the notion that emotions are not static but that they change over time and in response to external factors.

An example
Before sitting a test in class, Peter was feeling nervous because he did not know what to expect and he was unsure whether he would be able to complete the test successfully. After

the test Peter felt relieved because he had been able to attempt most of the questions. Therefore, Peter had recognised that the test was a trigger to changing his feelings. This may help him to predict his likely emotional responses in future tests.

Recognise simultaneous feelings in self

The ability to recognise simultaneous feelings involves appreciating that feelings can be complex and cannot always be described as comprising one emotion. It also involves being aware of a range of emotions and that they can occur concurrently as well as sequentially. Simultaneous feelings can work together as in the case of happiness and excitement or against each other as in the case of jealousy and happiness. Simultaneous feelings that seemingly contradict each other are the most difficult to deal with.

An example

Jane was invited to Jill's birthday party and took a cuddly teddy as a present. When she arrived at the party she felt happy to have been invited and excited to be giving Jill a present that she liked so much. At the same time Jane was also feeling resentful at having to give the present rather than keeping it for herself and jealous of all of the presents that Jill had already received.

The ability to hide feelings from others

The ability to hide feelings from others requires a good understanding of the verbal and non-verbal expressions of emotions (for example, tone of voice, body language, facial expression) and the ability to apply this knowledge. It also involves the ability to recognise the feeling(s) being experienced and those you wish to portray. It is important that children are aware of times when it is desirable or useful to hide their feelings from others.

An example

Billy arrives at school feeling very excited about his forthcoming holiday to Florida and cannot wait to tell his friend the good news. When he sees his friend come into the classroom crying, Billy hides his feelings of excitement and comforts his friend after learning that his hamster has died.

The ability to recognise likely emotional transitions

The ability to recognise likely emotional transitions involves an understanding that feelings can change to include the notion of likely sequences. These sequences will vary for each individual but it is important that individuals are aware of their own likely emotional transitions.

An example

Mary, a Year 6 child with emotional and behavioural difficulties, often loses her temper in class. After such an incident Mary tends to feel both ashamed and embarrassed. Making Mary aware of this likely emotional transition could be used to help her manage her behaviour, as reminders of the emotional consequences of her actions could be enough to alleviate some of the problematic behaviours.

The ability to take personal responsibility for our own emotions

The ability to take personal responsibility for our own emotions requires an understanding of the role that emotions play in our everyday lives and the impact that they have on both ourselves and others. It is important that we own our feelings at all times. In order to take responsibility for our emotions it is necessary to apply our understanding of all of the skills outlined in this section. Children should be encouraged to take responsibility for their emotions regardless of their stage of emotional development. There is an important link between managing emotions and taking responsibility for them. It is easier to manage our emotions if we take responsibility for them.

An example

Elliot was waiting in the dinner queue and a boy who he did not like elbowed him as he went past. This made Elliot feel angry but, instead of externalising this anger and saying that it was all the other boy's fault, Elliot was able to take responsibility for feeling like this. This places Elliot in a better position to manage his emotion.

Recognising and Understanding Emotions in Self (Self-awareness)

Nursery and Reception

Objective 1: **Encouraging the children to remain open to their feelings and to consider them throughout the day.**

Suggested activities

Use sad or happy cards (Appendix1, p. 97) for the children to display their emotions during the day. For example, children may be asked to hold up the card that describes how they are feeling during registration or place their Velcro name badge under the appropriate card. These cards may also be used during Circle Time.

Discuss pictures found in any books in the classroom, asking the children how the characters in the pictures or stories may feel. Discuss how characters on television programmes watched in nursery or school are feeling, focusing on the emotions of happy and sad.

Allow two minutes at the end of the day when the children can share any happy or sad memories of the day.

Make available happy or sad face badges or stickers for children to wear when they are feeling particularly happy or sad and want to share this with others. Initially teachers may need to ask why a child wearing a happy or sad badge feels this way. Following this it is hoped that the other children would begin to ask these questions of their peers.

Objective 2: **Developing a knowledge and understanding of the emotions of happy or sad.**

Suggested activities

Create a class 'happy' and 'sad' display detailing times when class members have felt happy and sad. The display could be illustrated with portraits of children feeling happy or sad and accompanying speech bubbles, 'Raj feels happy when...'

Discussion relating to the emotions of happy and sad

Much of this work could be covered during Circle Time using activities such as:

- Sentence completion: 'I feel happy when...', 'I feel sad when...'

- Silent activities such as 'pass the smile' when children smile and turn to the person sitting next to them which is then passed on to the next person in the circle or using silent statements such as 'everyone who feels happy today change places.' Discussion can then focus on why these children are feeling happy.

Stories and cartoons (where emotions may be exaggerated) may be used to help children to recognise the emotion and then relate it to their own experiences.

Expression of emotions through painting and drawing

Encourage children to consider the colours, facial expressions, body language and events associated with the emotions of happy and sad and use drawing and painting to convey this information. The theme of happy or sad could be given to the painting area for one week to provide a focus for the children's artwork. This could then be discussed during a Circle Time activity where children are invited to share their work, thus providing yet another stimulus for discussion.

Children can create a collage by cutting out pictures from magazines and catalogues of things that make them feel happy or sad. Teachers may wish to collate the cuttings into an appropriate shape, for example, a smile or a sad mouth. Discussions with the children regarding what they associate with feeling happy or sad may provide further ideas for the overall shape of the collage.

Recognising and Understanding Emotions in Self (Self-awareness)

Year 1

Objective 1: **Developing a knowledge and understanding of the emotions of angry, scared or excited.**

Suggested activities

Discussion relating to the emotions of angry, scared and excited. Much of this work could be covered during Circle Time using activities such as:

- Sentence completion: 'I feel angry when… (Mum will not give me a sweet)', 'When I feel scared I… (run to my Mum)', 'I know that I am feeling excited because… (I get butterflies in my tummy)'.

- Silent activities: using silent statements such as 'everyone who has felt scared today change places.' Discussion can then focus on why these children felt scared. Other activities such as passing the scared, angry or excited face around the circle may also be used.

Stories and cartoons (where emotions may be exaggerated) may be used to help children to recognise the emotion and then relate it to their own experiences.

Songs, rhymes or music may be used to reinforce the children's self-awareness of emotions already developed through other activities. For example, the class may create their own verses to the tune of *If you're happy and you know it clap your hands* to 'give a smile', 'do a dance', or 'if you're angry and you know it stamp your feet, give a scowl, clench your fists, etc.'

Puppet shows related to children's own experiences of emotions, for example, Emo's angry afternoon, Emo's happy half hour, Emo's exciting experience. Teachers and children could create their own scripts and these puppet shows could also be used as a stimulus for discussion during Circle Time.

Objective 2: Developing an ability to recognise an increased range of emotions in themselves.

Suggested activities

Children to choose a card from a series of pictures depicting various feelings (Appendix 2, p. 98). The children could use these pictures to show their feelings at the start of the day, possibly sticking these onto a chart (Appendix 3, p. 99) (maybe on their desk). This could then be changed as and when appropriate throughout the day, encouraging children to reflect on, and monitor, their own emotions.

A rainstick or tambourine could be used as a cue to prompt and encourage the children to reflect on their feeling of the moment. This may be particularly useful after playtimes so that a brief period of time can be set aside for reflection, following which the children are likely to be able to focus better on the content of the lesson.

Objective 3: Encouraging children to talk about their own emotional experiences.

Suggested activities

'Feelings flash' Time could be set aside at the start and end of the week (Monday a.m.; Friday p.m.) when the class (led by class teacher) could brainstorm events during the week or weekend that have resulted in various emotions. This runs on the same principles as a 'news flash' on the television. The feelings flash could be accompanied by a 'theme tune' that the children have composed.

Objective 4: Children to begin developing the ability to recognise their own personal triggers to various emotions.

Suggested activities

Sentence completion activities could be included during Circle Time, such as 'I feel ... when...'

Children could be asked to match a range of situation cards (Appendix 4, p. 100) to a choice of emotion cards (Appendix 5, p. 101). For example, they could match up the situation card of a fight at playtime with the emotion card of feeling angry, or they could match the situation card of their football going through the window with the emotion card of feeling scared. If a puppet character of Emo has been adopted, instead of using emotion cards, an Emo backpack could be made for each emotion so that the children could post the appropriate situation card into the appropriate backpack.

When using a rainstick or tambourine to mark a period of reflection (as outlined above), the activity could be extended to include the teacher asking the children to consider what has led them to experience the emotion. A progression of this activity could include the children discussing the trigger to their identified emotion when hearing the rainstick or tambourine.

Recognising and understanding Emotions in Self (Self-awareness)

Year 2

Objective 1: **Developing a knowledge and understanding of the emotions of worried, loved, bored or lonely.**

Suggested activities

Discussion relating to the emotions of worried, loved, bored and lonely. Much of this work could be covered during Circle Time using activities such as:

- Sentence completion: 'I feel bored when… (my teacher talks for a very long time)', 'When I feel worried I… (stay very quiet)', 'I know that I am feeling loved because… (I get a warm, calm feeling inside me)'.

- Silent activities such as using silent statements including 'everyone who has felt bored today change places.' Discussion can then focus on why these children felt bored.

Children could make a mobile of words with same or similar meanings for each emotion. For example:

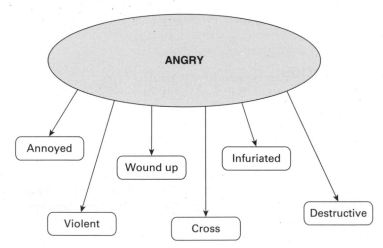

Children could begin to write their own short stories based on their own experiences of a given emotion. They may include events related to the emotion (trigger) and their own actions. These short stories could be collated into a class book of stories relating to a certain emotion, which could be used in other classes throughout the school or used as a stimulus for Circle Time discussion.

Children could create a class/individual recipe book for each of the feelings covered to date. For example, Emo's recipe for love could include; two arms to hug me, a pair of lips to kiss me... Emo's recipe for anger could include: three people not listening to me, two feet to kick with, a pinch for someone telling me 'no'...

During the summer term it may be appropriate to focus on the emotion of worried in order to discuss feelings related to SATs.

Objective 2: **Developing an understanding that all emotions are valid, recognising an increased range of emotions in themselves and remaining open to their emotions.**

Suggested activities

Children may use a 'feelings diary' (Appendix 6, p.102)) as a tool to encourage them to reflect on their feelings and have the confidence to validate these through the use of their diary. Children could be encouraged to complete simple diary entries regularly, as felt appropriate. These entries may be in the form of words or pictures, depending on the child's preferred mode of recording. At such times children should be encouraged to identify their emotion(s) and receive reassurance from the teacher/peers that their identified emotion is a valid one, whether it is positive or negative. A lot of class discussion may initially be required in order for children to begin to recognise that all emotions are valid. Children could also be asked to reflect on the trigger to their emotion in order to consolidate earlier work. An example of a diary entry is shown below:

Monday 29th February

How do I feel? Sad

Why do I feel sad? My grandad died at the weekend

Is it OK to feel sad? Yes

The children's understanding that all feelings are valid could be reinforced through the children making a class logo, poster or bookmark to act as a visual reminder that this is the case.

As in Year 1, time could be set aside at the start and end of the week (Monday a.m.; Friday p.m.), or on a daily basis, when the class (led by class teacher) could brainstorm events during the day, week or weekend that have resulted in various emotions. This runs on the same principles as a 'news flash' on the television. The feelings flash could be accompanied by a 'theme tune' that the children have composed. In Year 2 the 'feelings flash' could emphasise an increasing range of emotions and focus on validating **all** emotions.

Objective 3: **Children to begin developing the ability to recognise cues to their own emotions.**

Suggested activities

Discussion relating to recognising cues to emotions (how children know that they are experiencing a particular emotion). Much of this work could be covered during Circle Time using activities such as:

Sentence completion: 'How do you know when you are feeling...?' (I know that I am feeling loved because I get a warm, calm feeling inside me).

'If you can feel your heart beating fast, your palms getting sweaty and your muscles getting tense, how are you feeling?' (Angry.)

The children could brainstorm or share the cues that they recognise to their emotions, for example, butterflies when feeling excited, wanting to cry when feeling upset, wanting to jump up and down when feeling happy or excited and stamping feet when feeling angry etc.

The children could produce a class display reinforcing cues to various emotions. This may be achieved through either taking digital photographs of the children exaggerating a particular emotion and labelling ways in which they would know that they were experiencing this emotion. Alternatively a picture of Emo experiencing a particular emotion could be used and labelled according to how Emo will know how he is feeling.

For example: A display for the emotion of 'excited' may be similar to the one below.

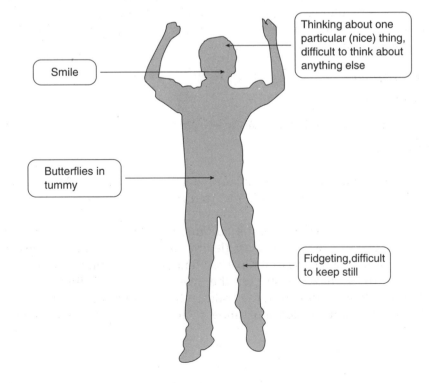

Recognising and Understanding Emotions in Self (Self-awareness)

Year 3

Objective 1: **Developing a knowledge and understanding of the emotions of shyness, frustration or contentment.**

Suggested activities

Stories, DVDs and cartoons (where emotions may be exaggerated) may be used to help children to recognise these emotions and relate them to their own experiences.

News reports and newspaper or magazine articles relating to real life events, such as tsunamis, earthquakes or hurricanes may provide a starting point for reflecting on emotions such as those of grief and frustration. These can then be related to their own experiences.

Discussion relating to the emotions of frustration, shyness and contentment. Much of this work could be covered during Circle Time using activities such as:

- Sentence completion: This may focus on identifying situational triggers to emotions, by using statements such as 'I feel frustrated when…', or may focus on actions evoked as a result of a certain emotion, by using statements such as 'When I feel shy, I…', or may focus on identifying cues to emotions, by using statements such as 'I know that I am feeling content because…' .

- Silent activities using silent statements such as 'everyone who has been frustrated today change places.' Discussion can then focus on the events that led to them feeling this way.

Songs, rhymes or music may be used to reinforce the children's self-awareness of emotions already developed through other activities. They may listen to pieces of music, such as Holst's *Planet Suite* and try to identify emotions portrayed within the music. Similarly the children may listen to the words contained within the lyrics of a song and relate these to their own experiences. Following on from this, children could be given the opportunity to create their own piece of music to portray an emotion or write song lyrics relating to a particular emotion. These could then be shared with the rest of the class.

Children could be given the opportunity to produce calligrams for various emotions and in doing this consider what a particular emotion means to them. For example, the children may choose to write the word angry using large, red, spiky, angular writing.

Children may write poetry or acrostic poems relating to the range of emotions covered to date. In doing this children may focus on their own experiences, their personal triggers to emotions, their actions as a result of emotions or cues to how they are feeling. Poems written by others may be a useful starting point.

Objective 2: **Continuing to develop the ability to reflect on, and recognise, a range of emotions within themselves.**

Suggested activities

'A feelings box' may provide further opportunities for developing the skills associated with self-awareness and reflection. A feelings box may be created by very simply decorating a shoebox and putting a posting hole in the top. Children can then be encouraged to post notes or pictures into the box to describe how they are feeling at a particular time (it may be useful if entries have the child's name written on the back). This could be used as a mechanism for sharing and validating emotions. At certain times during the day/week the box could be emptied and the children given the opportunity to discuss the contents of the box. For example, if Harry had posted a sad face into the box, the teacher may ask the rest of the children if they know why Harry may be feeling sad or may ask Harry what had made him feel sad. This can then lead to a discussion about what the class can do to help the child. So if Harry was feeling sad because he had no one to play with at playtimes maybe other children would offer to play with him. This should not devalue the emotion that Harry has been feeling but rather looks to address issues that may be both positive and negative.

Alternatively children could continue to use a diary as a way of encouraging them to recognise and record their range of emotions.

Objective 3: **Developing an awareness of the opportunity to engage or detach from emotions depending on their usefulness.**

Suggested activities

Various situations could be presented to the children. These might include: being given a present that you do not like, being shouted at by the teacher, being pushed into a swimming pool by your friend, finding a piece of work difficult or being scared of the dark. In pairs the children could then be given an opportunity to discuss the range of feelings that may be evoked by the given situation and to begin exploring the consequences of each of these feelings. From this the children could begin to identify which feelings are useful in which situation. For example:

Situation: finding a piece of work difficult.

Range of emotions: frustration, determination, upset, fear, anger, helplessness, ashamed, embarrassed, stupid, nervous, worried, pleased that you can not do any more or will receive help from the teacher.

Consequences of these emotions: Frustration may lead to an inability to work through the difficulty. Helplessness may lead to giving up. Being embarrassed may lead to completing the task in an inappropriate way or behaving in a silly manner. Determination may lead to perseverance. The most positive emotion in this situation would seem to be that of determination as this leads to the best outcome.

A similar exercise could be carried out using role play rather than discussion.

If the children are using a feelings diary (Appendix 7, p.103) then a column to focus on the usefulness of emotions they have felt could be included. This may be best completed the following day, after a period of reflection. A consideration of other more useful feelings in a given situation may also follow.

Objective 4: **Developing an understanding of the non-verbal expression of your own emotions.**

Suggested activites

The teacher may lead discussions relating to how emotions are displayed non-verbally. Pictures from newspapers/magazines or photographs could be used to initiate these discussions.

The children could play a game in pairs, miming the emotions displayed on a given card for their partner to guess. Following a guess, the child should be encouraged to give reasons for their choice of emotion, focusing primarily on the body language, facial expression and actions of the person that is miming.

The teacher may offer feedback to the children regarding their non-verbal expression of emotions so that the children can reflect on this for themselves. For example, if a child was sitting in class, rocking backwards and forwards on their chair while yawning and staring out of the window the teacher may comment on this suggesting that they are non-verbally expressing boredom. The child could then be encouraged to use this feedback positively in order to modify their behaviour(s). Once children get used to receiving this type of feedback they could be encouraged to provide it for each other in order to raise the awareness of children as to what they are communicating non-verbally.

Recognising and Understanding Emotions in Self (Self-awareness)

Year 4

Objective 1: **Developing a knowledge and understanding of the emotions of selfishness, disappointment, jealousy or unhappiness.**

Suggested activities

Discussion relating to the emotions of selfishness, disappointment, jealousy and feeling miserable. Much of this work could be covered during Circle Time using activities such as:

- Sentence completion: 'I feel miserable when...', 'When I feel disappointed I...' 'I know that I am feeling jealous because...'

- Silent statements: 'Everyone who has felt jealous today change places.' Discussion can then focus on why these children felt jealous.

In small groups children could be given the task of brainstorming as many situational triggers for these emotions as they can think of. These could then be shared with the rest of the class and used as the basis for class discussion in identifying the usefulness of the feeling within that particular situation.

The children could role-play non-verbally, the expression of the feelings focused on to date, by playing charades.

This knowledge could be consolidated by writing scripts for a puppet show. Further cross-curricular links could be developed by asking the children to design and make the puppets. Particular attention should be paid to the facial expression and body language of the puppets. The performance could be given to other classes throughout the school, thus providing a focus for further discussion.

The children could produce a 'mind map' using one of the above-mentioned emotions as a central focus.

Objective 2: **Recognition that feelings can change and reasons why this may occur.**

Suggested activities

Children could answer the register stating how they are feeling both in the morning and afternoon and give reasons for any change in feelings. For example, 'Good afternoon Miss. This morning I felt happy but now I'm feeling jealous because John spent playtime in the field with Sue and I wanted to play with him.'

Children could look at characters from cartoons, stories and films and discuss changes in the feelings of the characters and the reasons for the changes. Children could be encouraged to relate the changes identified to their own experiences.

The children could complete a diary or sheet to record changes in their feelings and reasons for those changes.

Objective 3: **Developing the ability to recognise physiological changes within themselves associated with various emotions.**

Suggested activities

When a person's emotions change this is often accompanied by a physiological change within the body. It is important that the children begin to learn about these changes and link the changes to their emotional state. For example, when feeling angry, a person's body releases adrenalin which results in an increased heartbeat, tensing of the muscles, increased energy levels and sweating amongst other changes which prepares the body for fight, flight or freeze.

In small groups, the children could draw around each other's body to produce an outline, which could then be labelled, in the appropriate places, with the physiological responses accompanying a particular emotion.

These posters could provide the basis for children to discuss their past experiences of these emotions. The teacher could then prompt the children to consider the physiological changes experienced at the same time as the emotion.

The children could spend time considering how cartoonists create emotions of their characters by highlighting and exaggerating the physiological changes that occur. Magazines, newspaper cuttings and animations may be used for this purpose. An example of this may be where a character is given hair standing on end, big eyes (pupils dilate to allow them to focus on the threat) and a white face (blood being directed towards the muscles to allow for flight or fight) to show fear.

If the children are using a feelings diary (Appendix 8, p.104) they may wish to create a space in which they can record any physiological changes that they identify. The feelings diary may look like the example below:

Date	Emotion	Trigger	Cue/Physiological change
23 January	Jealousy	New baby	Tense muscles, narrowed eyes, short temper

Objective 4: **Developing an understanding of the relationship between thoughts, feelings and actions.**

Suggested activities

Children could be given a range of cards (Appendix 9, p.105) including action cards, (Appendix 10, p.106) thought cards and feelings cards (Appendix 5, p.101). In pairs the children could be encouraged to match the cards and explain to another pair why they have put their cards together. For example:

Thought card (Appendix 10, p.106) they won't pick me next time and we lost the match because we only had ten players.

Action card being sent off football pitch for arguing with the referee.

Feeling card disappointment.

Once the children have become familiar with the cards they could make a set of their own, based on their own experiences.

The teacher could introduce the firework model of anger (Faupel, Herrick and Sharp, 1998) or similarly a 'kettle' model of anger, where the plug represents the trigger, the lead represents the thoughts which together result in the boiling of the water, which represents the physiological and behavioural actions associated with anger. Discussion can focus on the relationship between thoughts, feelings and actions and the children may design their own models for other emotions and share these with the rest of the class.

Recognising and Understanding Emotions in Self (Self-awareness)

Year 5

Objective 1: **Developing a knowledge and understanding of the emotions of guilt, grief, shame, pride, embarrassment or anger.**

Suggested activities

Discussion relating to the emotions of guilt, shame, pride, embarrassment and anger. Much of this work could be covered during Circle Time using activities such as:

- Sentence completion: 'I feel guilty when...', 'When I feel embarrassed I...' 'I know that I am feeling proud because...'

- Silent activities such as using silent statements including 'everyone who has felt proud today change places.' Discussion can then focus on why these children felt proud.

In small groups children could be given the task of brainstorming as many situational triggers for these emotions as they can think of. These could then be shared with the rest of the class and then be used as the basis for class discussion in identifying the usefulness of the feeling within that particular situation.

The children could create their own cartoons or cartoon characters depicting the non verbal and possibly physiological changes associated with these emotions.

They could consolidate this knowledge by writing scripts for a puppet show. Further cross-curricular links could be developed by asking the children to design and make the puppets. Particular attention should be paid to the facial expression and body language of the puppets. The performance could be given to other classes throughout the school, thus providing a focus for further discussion.

The children could brainstorm words of a similar meaning to the emotion(s) being focused on in order that they begin to see the relationship between emotions. A diagram such as that shown overleaf may provide a useful way of doing this.

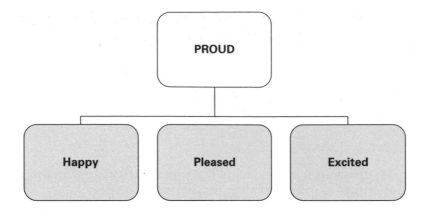

The children could also be encouraged to think about the relationship between the feelings of anger, embarrassment, pride and guilt and the resulting thoughts and actions. The children might do this in the form of the diagram below:

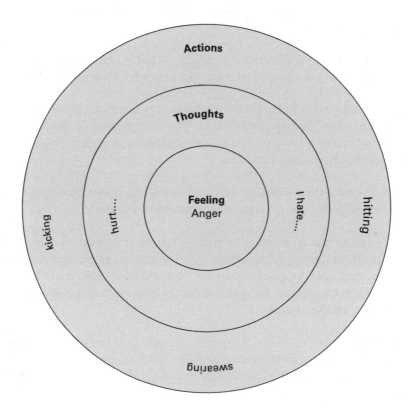

In order to help the children see the relationships between feelings children could be encouraged to group together feelings that lead to similar thoughts and actions.

Objective 2: **Developing an awareness of the possibility of hiding feelings and an ability to recognise this in themselves.**

Suggested activities

Use magazine pictures or short cuts taken from television programmes as a stimulus for discussing the emotion being portrayed in the picture or TV clip and any possible emotions that may be being hidden given knowledge gained from the background in the picture or the previous scenes in the video clip.

The children could be given pictures of people expressing a certain emotion and in pairs or small groups the children could fill in a speech bubble near the person with a range of possible feelings that may be being hidden and why this may be the case.

A focus for discussion during Circle Time may relate to the children considering when it may be helpful and when it may be unhelpful to hide their feelings. For example, it may be helpful to hide your own feelings of excitement and happiness if you know that your best friend's pet had just died. Similarly it may not be so helpful to hide your feelings if you are becoming more and more frustrated because you do not know how to complete a piece of work when the teacher is there to help you. During this discussion children could think about their own personal experiences of hiding their feelings and share these with their peers. If the child felt comfortable the class could then discuss whether they feel it was useful to hide or show their emotions in the situation described.

The teacher may like to consider creating an anonymous or private feelings box and once again an old shoebox could be used. The children can then be given the opportunity to record anonymously (or if they prefer with their name included), on a regular basis, feelings that they have hidden from others, how they did this and the outcome. These could then provide a stimulus for discussion during Circle Time as well as providing children with real examples of when this has occurred so that they are better able to recognise when they are doing it themselves. Whilst engaging in such work, which could be quite personal for the children, it is essential that the teacher talks to the class about the importance of respecting others' feelings and their need for privacy.

Objective 3: **Developing the ability to recognise the existence of simultaneous feelings in self.**

Suggested activities

The children could list their life events, which may include moving house, the death of family member or pet, SATs, the birth of a baby brother or sister, birthdays, Christmas or holidays, and then plot them into chronological order onto a 'life road'. The children could use words or pictures and a variety of colours to list these and the feelings associated with each event. Children should be encouraged to consider carefully whether they were experiencing more than one feeling during the events included on their life road. An example of a life road, including feelings is shown below:

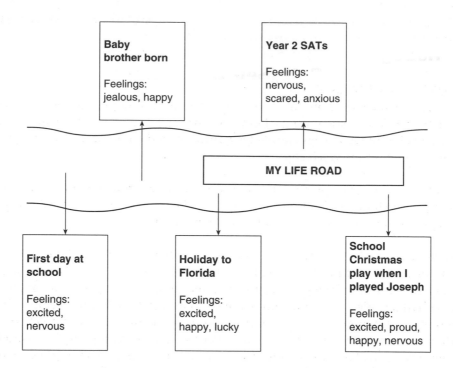

The children's life roads can be used as a stimulus for class or small group discussions about expression of simultaneous feelings and children could consider whether feelings experienced simultaneously are similar or dissimilar feelings. The teacher should be aware that some children may not wish to share their life roads with others and in this case the child's wish should be respected. The child may wish to talk to the teacher alone about their life road and that may be more appropriate in some instances.

Recognising and Understanding Emotions in Self (Self-awareness)

Year 6

Objective 1: **Developing a knowledge and understanding of the emotions of rejection, intimidation, arrogance and grief.**

Suggested activities

Discussion relating to the emotions of rejection, intimidation, arrogance and grief. Much of this work could be covered during Circle Time using activities such as:

- Sentence completion: 'I feel intimidated when...', 'When I feel rejected I...' 'I know that I am feeling grief because...'

- Activities using silent statements such as, 'Everyone who has felt rejected today change places.' Discussion can then focus on why these children felt rejected.

In small groups children could be given the task of brainstorming as many situational triggers for these emotions as they can think of. These could then be shared with the rest of the class and used as the basis for class discussion in identifying the usefulness of the feeling within that particular situation.

The children could create their own cartoons or cartoon characters depicting the non-verbal and possibly physiological changes associated with these emotions.

Children could consolidate this knowledge by writing scripts for a puppet show. Further cross-curricular links could be developed by asking the children to design and make the puppets. Particular attention should be paid to the facial expression and body language of the puppets. The puppet show could then be performed to other classes throughout the school.

The children could brainstorm words of a similar meaning to the emotion(s) being focused on, in order that they begin to see the relationship between emotions.

Discussion could focus around the role of these and other emotions in learning and how useful they are in the process of learning. During the course of a week children could be encouraged to keep a note of the emotions experienced when pieces of work they perceive as being of good quality are completed; and also keep a note of the emotions experienced when they struggle to complete a piece of work. These notes could then provide the basis for a class discussion, during which the relationship between feelings, thoughts and actions (work) could also be discussed.

The children should be given the opportunity to discuss how these feelings may be hidden and in which situations this may be desirable. Discussion should encourage the children to focus on, and share, their own experiences.

Discussion should also provide children with the opportunity to identify feelings that may occur simultaneously with the emotions of grief, rejection, arrogance and intimidation. Again children should be encouraged to focus on their own experiences and giving children situations may be helpful in initiating this kind of thinking. For example, if given the scenario of attending a funeral, children may respond by saying that they could experience both grief and relief at the same time; grief because someone has died and relief because the person/pet was ill and they are no longer suffering and in pain.

Objective 2: **Encouraging children to begin taking personal responsibility for reflecting on and managing their emotions.**

Suggested activites
Children should be given the opportunity to choose their preferred method of recording/reflecting on their own emotions from those strategies used in previous years. These include:

- Board to display feelings on.

- Post box.

- Diary.

- Private feelings file.

- Or, at this stage, children may choose to internalise this.

When using these methods for recording/reflecting on emotions children should be encouraged to accept personal responsibility for their emotions. They should also be encouraged to recognise that their emotions are legitimate (it may also still be helpful to encourage the children to identify the triggers to these emotions) but that it is their responsibility to manage these emotions and not allow them significantly negatively to affect their daily routines. At this stage the relationship between this activity and the work completed during the 'self regulation of emotions' strand should be made explicit.

Objective 3: **Developing the ability to recognise likely transitions between feelings in themselves.**

Suggested activites
Children should be encouraged to recognise how feelings change and in doing this be able to identify how their emotions are likely to change. The following activities may help the children to develop this skill.

Providing the children with random lists of emotions and encouraging them to work in pairs discussing likely transitions (Appendix 11, pp. 107–108) from the given emotion based on own experiences. For example, if presented with the emotion of 'anger' one likely transition is to that of 'guilt', as after an angry outburst people often then feel guilty about their actions which may result in apologies or crying.

The children could also engage in a role play where they are given two cards with different emotions on them. The children then have to think of a scenario that may result in the transition from the first emotion to the second emotion and create a role play to demonstrate the transition between the two emotions. These role plays could then be shared with the rest of the class who have to try and identify the first emotion, the trigger to the change in emotions and the second emotion.

Particular attention should be given to the likely transitions between feelings involved in processes of grief and anger as these strong emotions often result in a whole series of emotions experienced over time.

Objective 4: **Developing the ability to recognise the importance of emotion in learning.**

Suggested activites

Children should be encouraged to recognise the important role that emotions have to play in the process of learning through discussion of personal experiences. Following an initial discussion the following activities could be used to reinforce the effect of emotions on learning.

After practice SATs papers children could be given the opportunity to discuss the emotions that they experienced and the effects of these on their performance and learning. The experience of practice SATs papers is likely to exaggerate the role of emotions in learning, however these findings could then be generalised to all learning within the classroom.

Children could also be given the task of brainstorming as many emotions as they possibly can. Following this the children could be asked to sort these emotions into three groups depending on whether they have a positive/negative/neutral effect on learning. The children could then share this information either in small groups or as a whole class and use this to stimulate further discussion about personal experiences and the role of emotions in learning.

The children could produce slogans/posters highlighting the emotions that promote learning or academic risk taking in the classroom. These could then be displayed and provide a visual reminder as to the range of emotions that are productive to learning.

4

Recognising and Understanding Emotions in Others

The ability to recognise and understand emotions in others involves interpreting other people's verbal and non-verbal signals. This emotional competence develops from the recognition of basic emotions in others, such as happiness and sadness, to abilities such as empathy. This strand provides the foundations upon which higher order social skills are based. A suggested progression of the competencies involved in recognising and understanding emotions in others is outlined below. They include the ability to:

o   Recognise basic emotions in others.
o   Recognise cues to others' emotions.
o   Recognise others' triggers to emotions.
o   Recognise the effects of our own emotion/behaviour on the emotions of others (and vice-versa).
o   Engage with and detach from others' emotions.
o   Demonstrate empathy for others.
o   Recognise changes in others' emotions and relate these to events where appropriate.
o   Recognise simultaneous feelings in others.

Each of these competencies will now be considered individually and examples given of children demonstrating the skill. It is important to remember that because children learn from 'significant others' you as the teacher will be modelling the competencies for the children. Explicit modelling of these skills, including verbally describing what you are doing or have done, will be beneficial for the children.

The ability to recognise basic emotions in others

The ability to recognise basic emotions (happiness and sadness) in others involves children being able to look at, and listen to, another person and then both identify and label the emotion that they think the other person is experiencing. Children will need to have developed the ability to recognise these emotions in themselves before they can accurately recognise them in others.

An example
Ranjit is playing a game of football with his friend when his friend scores a goal. Ranjit is able to recognise his friend's emotion as happiness because he knows that he feels happy when he scores a goal. Ranjit also relates his friend's smile and celebratory behaviour as being associated with the emotion of feeling happy.

The ability to recognise cues to others' emotions
The ability to recognise cues to others' emotions involves looking carefully at facial expression and body posture as well as listening to the words spoken by the other person and the tone of their voice. Children who are developing this skill will need practice in observing others as this is the only way that they can begin to interpret body language and facial expression. Children who have developed this skill will have the ability to determine how a person is feeling by interpreting the verbal and non-verbal messages that they observe and hear. They will have created associations between certain behaviours and certain emotions which assist them in recognising others' emotions.

An example
Sarah was walking to school with her mum and little brother, James. James ran ahead towards the road. As Sarah's mum screamed 'James stop' Sarah looked at her mum's wide-eyed face and realised that she was scared because James may have run across the road. Sarah was able to do this as she had made an association between the emotion of scared and the tone of voice and words used, and the facial expression of an open mouth and wide eyes.

The ability to recognise others' triggers to emotions and our role in these
A trigger is the event that elicits an emotion. The ability to recognise triggers to the emotions of others involves relating an event to the emotion of a person. This skill is developed from combining our knowledge of triggers to our own emotions with an understanding that others may feel different emotions from any given trigger. This skill therefore involves expanding the associations made between triggers and emotions in ourselves to include a wider range of emotions that may be experienced by others in response to the same trigger.

An example
At playtime Ameena told Nisha that she could not join in their game. When they returned to the classroom Ameena noticed that Nisha was crying. Ameena thought that the trigger to Nisha's unhappiness was leaving her out of the game at playtime. As a result of this Ameena apologised to Nisha and asked her if she would like to play with them at lunchtime.

This situation also resulted in Ameena recognising that being left out of a game can result in people feeling unhappy or lonely. Until this time Ameena had only really associated being left out of one game with going to play with someone else as this trigger did not result in the same emotions for Ameena.

The ability to recognise the effects of one's own emotions or behaviour on the emotions of others

The ability to recognise how our own emotions or behaviour affects others involves the recognition that through our behaviour, we can be a trigger to, or cause of, another person's emotions. Children who have developed this skill will be able to appreciate the causal relationship between them/their behaviour and the emotion of another.

An example

Carla was shouting out and tapping her pencil on the table while her teacher was trying to teach a maths lesson. Carla's teacher started to get annoyed and asked Carla to stop shouting out and tapping her pencil because it was making him feel annoyed. Carla then realised that her behaviour was affecting the emotions of the teacher and that she was acting as the trigger to his emotions.

Developing the ability to engage with or detach from others' emotions

The ability to choose to engage with, or detach from, others' emotions involves an awareness that this can be either helpful or unhelpful and is a skill that is likely to take a long time to develop and requires a lot of practice. The knowledge that engaging with, or detaching from, others' emotions can be helpful or unhelpful then needs to be applied in order to make an informed choice about your own actions. It may be more appropriate to engage with, or detach from, the emotions of another person in part. In doing this the feeling of the other person is acknowledged and validated but it is not overwhelming. Personal experience of having attached to the emotions of another too much or too little is likely to be a key factor in developing this skill.

An example

Richard arrives in school one day very upset because his hamster had died over the weekend. Elliot recognised that Richard was feeling upset and chose to attach in part to this feeling so that he could be sympathetic towards Richard but did not fully attach with the feeling as he thought that he would get very upset himself.

Developing the ability to demonstrate empathy for others

The ability to demonstrate empathy for others involves recognising the emotions of others, recalling a time that you felt a similar emotion and what it was like to feel that way and then acting in an appropriate way towards the other person. Empathy requires that you put yourself into the shoes of another and act in the way that you would like someone to act towards you in the same situation. Empathy involves sharing (to some extent) an experience with someone else.

An example

Emma was named as 'star of the week' in assembly and collected a certificate from the headteacher. Victoria, Emma's friend recognised that Emma was feeling very proud because that is how she had felt when she was given the 'star of the week' award. After the assembly Victoria went up to Emma and congratulated her, thus sharing in her enjoyment.

Developing the ability to recognise changes in others' emotions and relate these changes to events

The ability to recognise changes in the emotions of others involves a knowledge that emotions can change over time and in response to events. It involves having an awareness of the emotions of people around you, so that changes in verbal and non-verbal behaviours can be identified. Following a specific event, emotions can be heightened or there can be an increased likelihood of them changing. As a consequence of this we may monitor the emotions of those around us more closely following an event, so that changes in emotion are identified early and we can empathise with the person.

An example

Mohammad and Matthew were sitting in the classroom talking happily about what they had done at the weekend. The teacher then read out the results of the spelling test from the Friday before and Matthew found out that he had only got 1 out of 10. Mohammad recognised that Matthew no longer felt happy but that he now felt embarrassed at his low score.

Developing the ability to recognise simultaneous feelings in others

The ability to recognise simultaneous feelings in others involves the knowledge that people can experience more than one emotion at any one time. This skill involves extending the ability to recognise simultaneous emotions in yourself to recognising them in others. There also needs to be an appreciation that the range of emotions experienced at the same time differs from person to person.

An example

It was the final day in primary school for Anna and Sarah who had both really enjoyed their time at school. Anna noticed that although Sarah was laughing she looked upset and slightly anxious. When Anna asked Sarah if she was OK, Sarah said that even though she was having a nice day and had lots of happy memories of school she was upset that she had to leave and a bit worried about going to a big secondary school where she would not know anyone.

Recognising and Understanding Emotions in Others

Nursery and Reception

Objective 1: **Developing the ability to recognise in others the emotions of happy and sad.**

Suggested activities

Ask the children to find pictures of people that look happy and sad in magazines and newspapers. The children can then cut these pictures out and make a class collage.

The children could use a digital camera to take photographs of class members looking happy and sad. These can be made into a display and discussed.

The children should be given the opportunity to consider how the teacher or other members of the class may be feeling at a given time. This type of discussion could take place during a structured time such as Circle Time or incidentally as it arises. In addition to identifying the emotion children could be encouraged to try and think about why the person might feel happy or sad.

During story time or when children are looking at books they should be encouraged to consider the feelings of the characters. The teacher could prompt the children to look for a particular emotion when looking at books independently, by placing a happy or sad face in the book corner.

Children could be encouraged to engage in role play activities where the focus is placed on experiencing an emotion within a safe environment and interpreting other people's emotions within the same setting. To encourage this type of role play children may need to be given scenarios. For example, to encourage children to identify feelings of happiness in others, role play scenarios may include a birthday party, going on holiday or buying a new toy. Possible scenarios focusing on identifying the feeling of sadness in others may include losing a pet or not being collected from school on time by their parents. These same scenarios could be used as stimuli for puppet shows too.

Children can be encouraged to act out nursery rhymes in which the characters are either happy or sad during role play activities in a 'nursery rhyme corner' within the classroom. Nursery rhymes chosen to focus on the emotion of happiness may include *Hey-diddle-diddle*, *Mary Mary quite contrary* or *Five currant buns in a baker's shop*. Nursery rhymes that could be acted out that focus on the emotion of sadness may include *Little Bo-Peep*, *Cock Robin*, *Humpty Dumpty* and *Old Mother Hubbard*.

Recognising and Understanding
Emotions in Others

Year 1

Objective 1: **Developing the ability to recognise in others an increasing range of emotions including angry, scared or excited.**

Suggested activities

Class discussions could centre on the emotions of angry, scared and excited. Much of this work could be covered during Circle Time using activities such as:

- Sentence completion: 'I can tell when ... is feeling angry because ... (her face goes red and she starts to shout)'. 'When ... is feeling excited she ... (jumps up and down and flaps her hands)'.

During story time, or when children are looking at books, they should be encouraged to consider the feelings of the characters. They could be directed to look for a particular emotion when looking at books or asked to suggest a book for a class story that they think portrays one of the targeted emotions.

The character of Emo could be used for the children to practice recognising emotions. The class could make a 'feelings face' based on Emo. A face would need to be cut from cardboard. The children could then make sets of eyes and mouths depicting different emotions which could be stuck onto the face using either blu-tac or velcro. Other features could be made as appropriate and may include colours for cheeks, nose or hair.

Objective 2: **Developing the ability to recognise and use cues to others' emotions.**

Suggested activities

Games based on mime: the children could be given a selection of cards with emotions written on them (Appendix 5, p.101). The children can then take it in turns to choose a card and mime this to the other children, who have to guess what the emotion is. The focus of the miming could change; it could focus only on facial expression or body language. This will enable the children to develop the ability to recognise emotions in others using a variety of cues.

Emotion cue cards (Appendix 5, p.101) could be used again but this time the focus for the children could be placed on the tone of voice being used. This will encourage the children to use this as another cue to recognising the emotions of others. The children could take it in turns to choose an emotion card and then use this to sing a nursery rhyme using a tone of voice to match the chosen emotion. Other children could then guess the emotion. Toy telephones could be used in a similar way to reinforce this skill, allowing the children to practice recognising emotions from a person's voice.

A wall display could be created to summarise the various cues that can be used to recognise other people's emotions. The children could use large pictures of Emo or of any other character (this may be a character from history, cartoons or a story) and label these to demonstrate cues to others' emotions. The labels will need to focus on the character's body language, facial expression or tone of voice. This display could be accompanied by a statement summarising the cues used in the sentence 'We know …(character) is feeling … (emotion) because… (cues used to identify feeling).

If the 'feelings flash' outlined on in Chapter Three (Years One and Two) is used in class then it would be easy to add another element to this activity. Rather than just focusing on their own emotions, the children could now be encouraged to identify how the teacher is feeling and explain how they know this.

Encourage the children to begin noticing cues to emotions in their friends. The children could be paired up with a 'feeling buddy' in which case the buddy should be changed at regular intervals or this could be used as a class-wide activity. When a child has recognised an emotion they can approach the person by saying 'I think you're feeling _____'. If the friend is in agreement then a sticker/tick can be put on the class chart for recognition of feelings. This can then be discussed in Circle Time.

The children could make masks based on the character of Emo. These masks should depict a variety of emotions including happy, sad, scared, angry and excited. These masks could then be used in a structured context e.g. the children could be asked to choose the appropriate mask to illustrate the emotions of a character in a story (for example, during guided reading sessions). They could also be used during structured role play sessions where children are encouraged to take on the role of a character who expresses a particular emotion.

Recognising and Understanding
Emotions in Others

Year 2

Objective 1: **Developing the ability to recognise in others an increasing range of emotions including loved, bored and lonely.**

Suggested activities

Class discussions could centre on the emotions of loved, bored and lonely. Much of this work could be covered during Circle Time using activities such as:

- Sentence completion: 'I can tell when … is feeling lonely because … (she wanders around on her own looking unhappy)', 'When … is feeling bored he … (stares in space and yawns a lot)'.

- Silent statements: 'If you have seen someone looking lonely today stand up and swap places.' Those children that do swap places could be asked to explain how they recognised that someone was feeling lonely and what they did about it.

- Characters from familiar stories or rhymes could be used as the basis for discussion or sentence completion activities with the children needing to justify why they think the character is feeling a particular emotion.

In small groups, the children could create a puppet show where the characters portray a range of targeted emotions. When this puppet show has been performed to the rest of the class a discussion can follow about the emotions of the characters.

Objective 2: **Developing the ability to recognise others' triggers to emotions and our own role in this.**

Suggested activities

Familiar people, for example; a child's parent, carer, teacher or friend and other characters such as Emo, a favourite TV character, story character, sports star or pop star can be the focus for this activity. It may be helpful to have pictures of the characters during this activity. The children should be asked to name the present emotion and discuss what may have triggered this. If the person focused on during this activity is a carer, teacher or friend the children should be encouraged to consider their own role in triggering the emotion.

The children could be presented with a range of cards each outlining a different situation. These 'situation cards' (Appendix 4, p.100) could then be used as a basis for discussion or role play. The children could also play a guessing game trying to work out the range of emotions that may be triggered by the given situation.

The children could make a 'class cloud' to depict class triggers to emotions. This could hang from the ceiling and should recognise the role that class members play in eliciting emotions in others. The class cloud for the emotion of 'boredom' may look like this:

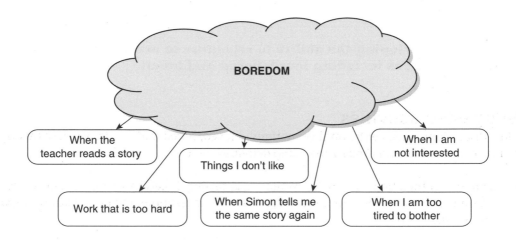

Recognising and Understanding Emotions in Others

Year 3

Objective 1: **Developing the ability to recognise in others an increasing range of emotions including shyness, frustration and relaxation.**

Suggested activities

Class discussions could centre on the emotions of shyness, grief, frustration and relaxation. Much of this work could be covered during Circle Time using activities such as:

- Sentence completion: 'I can tell when ... is feeling frustrated because ... (he bangs his fist on the desk and grimaces)', 'When ... is feeling relaxed she ... (hums quietly to herself and swings her legs under the chair as she reads her book'.

- Silent statements: 'If you have seen someone looking shy today stand up and swap places.' Those children that do swap places could be asked to explain how they recognised that someone was feeling shy and what they did about it.

- Characters from familiar stories or rhymes could be used as the basis for discussion/sentence completion activities with the children needing to justify why they think the character is feeling a particular emotion.

- Discussion during Circle Time could focus on the children identifying triggers to the target emotions. For example, if the target emotion was frustration, each child could be asked to think of the last time that they felt frustrated and identify the trigger that led to this feeling.

The children could discuss the usefulness of recognising emotions in others. They could be paired at the start of the day and asked to record the range of feelings that they notice in their partner during the morning. After lunch the children could then be asked to discuss their observations with their partner. The initial focus could be on establishing whether the emotion recorded was an accurate reflection of how their partner had been feeling. Then the children could discuss how useful they felt the feeling had been in the situation and how useful it was for them to be able to recognise the emotion in another person. For example, Paul and Debbie were paired up in the morning. Throughout the morning Debbie noted that Paul appeared to experience the following emotions: excited, frustrated, bored and nervous. After lunch Debbie shared these observations with Paul, who agreed that he had experienced these emotions during the morning. They then discussed how useful these emotions had been for Paul within the situation that had occurred. Paul and Debbie agreed that it wasn't useful for Paul to feel nervous during the maths test because this prevented him concentrating and working to the best of his ability. Debbie felt that on this occasion it was not particularly useful to have recognised that Paul was feeling this way as there was little that she could do about it in the test situation. It did however enable Debbie to empathise with him and be sympathetic in her response to him after the test.

One possible extension activity is for the children to be encouraged to use their knowledge of emotions in others to write stories. This will reinforce work covered during the teaching sessions as well as improving the children's ability to build up characters in stories.

Objective 2: **Beginning to recognise opportunities to engage with, or detach from, others' emotions.**

Suggested activities

The children could play a game based on snakes and ladders with decision points at the bottom of the ladder or the top of the snake requiring children to decide whether to engage with, or detach from, the emotion of another person in a given situation. A discussion could follow regarding the decision made, focusing on whether, given the situation, there is agreement about whether it is the better decision and therefore, whether the game continues, deciding how to move on in the game, i.e. move up the ladder or down the snake. For example, the situation described at the decision point may be that you are on holiday in Blackpool in the sea. Do you engage or detach from your sister's feeling of fear about sharks swimming in the sea? Discussion may include; the likelihood of there being sharks in the sea in Blackpool, is a little bit of fear good when you are in the sea because of it being so dangerous? Or whether your sister always feels frightened? Following this discussion the consensus may be that it would be better to detach from this emotion as there are not likely to be sharks in Blackpool and that your sister is frightened of so many things that this is not a rational fear in this situation. There is unlikely to be a right or wrong answer but it is important that the children are able to justify the answer given, demonstrating that they have considered a range of factors. This activity could be completed as a whole class activity or in small groups or pairs.

This activity is similar to the one described above but does not involve a game. Instead the children are just presented with a situation card (Appendix 4, p.100) and a feeling card (Appendix 5, p.101). The children then have to decide whether it would be useful for them to engage with, or detach from, the emotion and explain their reasons for this. A possible extension to this activity is for the children to devise the situations themselves based on their own experiences at home/school. This could form the basis of a Circle Time activity.

The children could engage in a class debate, focusing on a given situation (this situation could be chosen by either the teacher or a child). The class should be split in half, with half of the children arguing for attaching to the feeling and half arguing for detaching from the feeling. This debate could be used to explore a range of issues, to highlight the complexity of reaching decisions about emotions and to encourage the children to consider other people's viewpoints.

Recognising and Understanding Emotions in Others

Year 4

***Objective 1*: Developing the ability to recognise in others an increasing range of emotions including selfishness, disappointment, jealousy and feeling miserable.**

Suggested activities

Class discussions could centre on others' emotions of selfishness, disappointment, jealousy and feeling miserable. Much of this work could be covered during Circle Time using activities such as:

- Sentence completion: 'I can tell when ... is feeling jealous because...(she makes unkind comments and narrows her eyes)', 'When ... is feeling disappointed he ... (looks down and his voice sounds flat)'.

- Silent statements: 'If you have seen someone looking miserable today stand up and swap places.' Those children that do swap places could be asked to explain how they recognised that someone was feeling miserable and what they did about it.

- Characters from familiar TV programmes/DVDs could be used as the basis for discussion/sentence completion activities with the children needing to justify why they think the character is feeling a particular emotion.

- Discussion during Circle Time could focus on the children identifying triggers to the target emotions. For example, if the target emotion was jealousy, each child could be asked to think of the last time that they felt jealous and identify the trigger that led to this feeling.

- Discussing the usefulness of recognising emotions in others. Children could share times when they have recognised emotions in others which have been useful because they have been able to help. For example, if a child recognised that another child was feeling lonely they may have used this information in a positive way by asking them to play with them at playtime.

Objective 2: **Developing the ability to recognise the effect of one's own and others' behaviour on emotions.**

Suggested activities

The children could watch clips of cartoons and while watching the cartoons they could record the effects of one character's behaviour on another character's emotions. This information could then be shared and form the basis for discussion.

The children could create their own cartoons, depicting the effect of behaviour on the emotions of others. Using the cartoon format, emotions can be exaggerated with ease. Children could then share their cartoon with peers. This could be an individual, paired or small group activity.

The children should be encouraged to keep a record of their behaviour and how it affects others' emotions and consequently their behaviour. The recording of this information could be in symbols or pictures or words. The chart below provides an example of one way of recording this information using words.

My behaviour	Others' emotions/behaviour
I gave Robert a piece of my birthday cake	He felt happy and then played with me
I shouted at Claire because she wouldn't give me the rubber	She felt angry and hit me

Children could bring completed records to Circle Time and these could form the basis of a discussion, highlighting the positive and negative effects that our behaviour can have on other people.

Short periods of time (approximately 15–30 minutes) could be used for group work focussing on the effect our actions have on the emotions of others. Each group could be split in half. Half of the children could be given an action to model to the other half of the group. This may include 'being nice', 'being unkind' or 'being calm'. They should model the actions through the use of body language, facial expression and tone of voice. At the end of the session the children could describe how the behaviour of those following the instruction affected their emotions and actions. This can then be related to everyday situations to highlight the link between behaviour and the emotion of others.

Recognising and Understanding Emotions in Others

Year 5

Objective 1: **Developing the ability to recognise in others an increasing range of emotions including guilt, grief, shame, pride, embarrassment and anger.**

Suggested activities

Class discussions could centre on others' emotions of guilt, shame, pride, anger and embarrassment. Much of this work could be covered during Circle Time using activities such as:

- Sentence completion: 'I can tell when … is feeling proud because…(he smiles and shows the work that he is proud of to everyone)' 'When … is feeling embarrassed she … (looks down and her face starts to turn red)'.

- Silent statements: 'If you have seen someone looking angry today stand up and swap places.' Those children that do swap places could be asked to explain how they recognised that someone was feeling angry and what they did about it.

- Characters from familiar TV programmes or DVDs could be used as the basis for discussion and sentence completion activities with the children needing to justify why they think the character is feeling a particular emotion.

- Discussion during Circle Time could focus on the children identifying triggers to the target emotions. For example, if the target emotion was proud, each child could be asked to think of the last time that they observed someone else feeling proud and identify possible triggers that led to the other person experiencing this emotion.

- Discussing the usefulness of recognising emotions in others. Children could share times when they have recognised emotions in others which have been useful because they have been able to help. For example, if a child recognised that another child was feeling embarrassed they may have used this information in a positive way by reassuring them that things were OK. The focus of this activity should be on those target emotions listed above.

- Children could discuss how their behaviour may result in people feeling ashamed, proud, angry, embarrassed or guilty. The class may then discuss how the behaviour of other children in the class makes them feel.

- The children could discuss how people might hide feelings from them. They may first need to focus on how they may hide their own emotions from others and then generalise this knowledge.

Objective 2: **To develop children's awareness of empathy and their ability to demonstrate it.**

Suggested activities

Children should be encouraged to listen to others' points of view and acknowledge these during daily activities.

Children could be asked to write letters in response to 'problem page' (Appendix 12, pp. 109–110) type letters. The difficulties could be related to friendships, relationships with parents/carers or situational difficulties. The response of the children will require them to empathise with the author of the letter. The letters could be written in pairs, which will facilitate discussion of the problem and possible solutions. How do they feel and how can you help?

A peer mediation system could be set up to encourage the children to listen to others' points of view, acknowledge their feelings and offer support. Children could be identified and then trained as mediators and be made available to help others resolve conflicts within the class (see Stacey and Robinson 1997). Schrumpf, Crawford and Bodine (1997) suggest that peer mediation involves the following six steps:

Step 1   Agree to mediate
          Introductions
          State ground rules

Step 2   Gather points of view
          Ask each person what has happened
          Ask each person if they want to add anything

Step 3   Focus on interests
          Focus on common interests
          Determine and summarise shared interests

Step 4   Create win-win options
          Brainstorm solutions and ask those involved what could be done to resolve the problem

Step 5   Evaluate options and choose a solution
          Ask each person what can be done to resolve the conflict

Step 6   Create an agreement
          Write or agree a way forward
          Sign or shake hands on the agreement

If you are interested in setting up a peer mediation system within your class consultation with the Behaviour Support Service or Educational Psychology Service may help you.

Objective 3: **Developing the ability to recognise changes in others' emotions and relate these to events.**

Suggested activities

Different groups of children can focus on different characters while watching a film and create an emotion profile for their target character. Children can use the notes that they have made while watching the film to plot the changes in emotions of their character in relation to the different events in the film. These character emotion profiles can then be compared.

Recognising and Understanding Emotions in Others

Year 6

Objective 1: **Developing the ability to recognise in others an increasing range of emotions including rejection, intimidation, arrogance and grief.**

Suggested activities

Class discussions could centre on the emotions of rejection, intimidation, arrogance and grief in others. Much of this work could be covered during Circle Time using activities such as:

- Sentence completion: 'I can tell when … is feeling rejected because…(he isolates himself from everyone and looks sad)'. 'When … is feeling intimidated she … (turns away and mumbles)'.

- Silent statements: 'If you have seen someone looking rejected today stand up and swap places.' Those children that do swap places could be asked to explain how they recognised that someone was feeling rejected and what they did about it.

- Characters from familiar TV programmes or DVDs could be used as the basis for discussion and sentence completion activities with the children needing to justify why they think the character is feeling a particular emotion.

- Discussion during Circle Time could focus on the children identifying triggers to the target emotions. For example, if the target emotion was grief, each child could be asked to think of the last time that they observed someone else feeling grief-stricken and identify possible triggers that led to the other person experiencing this emotion.

- Discussing the usefulness of recognising emotions in others. Children could share times when they have recognised emotions in others which have been useful because they have been able to help. For example, if a child recognised that another child was feeling arrogant they may be able to use this information in a positive way by reassuring themselves that the other child's behaviour was unacceptable. The focus of this activity should be on those target emotions listed above.

- Children could discuss how their behaviour may result in people feeling rejected, arrogant, grief-stricken or intimidated. The class may then discuss how the behaviour of other children in the class makes them feel.

- The children could discuss how people might hide feelings from them. They may first need to focus on how they may hide their own emotions from others and then generalise this knowledge.

- The children could also discuss how they could show empathy for others displaying these feelings, particularly grief, intimidation and rejection.

Objective 2: **Developing the ability to recognise simultaneous feelings in others.**

Suggested activities

Children could be encouraged to watch news clips or study historical events and identify simultaneous feelings in the people concerned. For example, they may study life in the concentration camps during the second world war and consider the feelings of those held there. These feelings may include fear, grief, anxiety, hope, optimism and anger.

The children could role play interviews. One of the pair takes on the part of the interviewee and the other the part of the interviewer. The interviewee recounts an event (either from their own lives or from a given situation card) during which simultaneous emotions are experienced. The interviewer then tries to reflect the correct feelings back to the interviewee. This exercise could take the form of a 'Feelings Flash' format (see p.17 and Appendix 13, p.111).

5

Management and Regulation of Emotions

This strand recognises the importance of being able to manage our emotions. This emotional competence develops from beginning to recognise a need to take responsibility for our emotions, to the ability to re-frame situations that evoke emotions and use our emotions in a positive way. A suggested progression of the competencies involved in developing the management of emotions includes the ability to:

- o Begin taking responsibility for feelings.
- o Recognise the range of possible reactions to a variety of emotions and the subsequent need to manage our emotions.
- o Discriminate between appropriate and inappropriate expressions of emotions.
- o Understand the role of emotions in learning.
- o Manage the feelings of anger, fear, worry, loneliness, frustration and grief in an appropriate way.
- o Manage a variety of emotional states through the use of relaxation, calming techniques and visualisation.
- o Re-frame situations in a more positive way.
- o Manage the feelings of rejection, guilt, jealousy and anger (at a more complex level) in an appropriate way.
- o Use feelings in a positive way.

Each of these competencies will now be considered individually and examples are given of children demonstrating the skill. It is important to remember that because children learn from 'significant others', you as the teacher will be modelling the competencies for the children. Explicit modelling of these skills, including verbally describing what you are doing or have done, will be beneficial for the children.

The ability to begin taking responsibility for feelings

The ability to begin taking responsibility for our own feelings involves recognising and labelling our own emotions, developing an understanding that emotions belong to us and that we are able to use them in both positive and negative ways, which impacts on both ourselves and other people.

An example

Sanjay arrived in school on his birthday telling his teacher that he was feeling very excited because he was having a party after school. Sanjay's teacher explained that she was happy for him but she reminded him that even though it was his birthday he still needed to do some work in class, and that it was his responsibility to manage his feeling of excitement appropriately within school. The teacher may have helped him to achieve this by suggesting that he should only talk about his party during break times as otherwise he would not concentrate on the lessons.

An awareness of the need to manage our own emotions

The ability to recognise the need to manage our own emotions involves recognising the range of possible reactions to a variety of emotions. As this skill is developed the importance of learning how to manage our own emotions becomes evident. Children who have developed this skill will be able to describe how they may react when feeling a particular emotion. They will also understand that sharing an emotion in any circumstance may not always be appropriate and that certain expressions of emotions, such as hurting others when angry, are not appropriate.

An example

Samantha often gets into trouble in assembly at school. Samantha's teacher asked her why she often gets into trouble in assembly and Samantha reported that she feels bored because there is nothing to look at. When prompted by her teacher Samantha is able to identify the range of ways that she may react when she feels bored. She might shout out, play with her hair, take her shoes off or start giggling or making faces with a friend. Through discussion with her teacher, Samantha was able to understand that boredom is a valid emotion but that it requires careful management so that her emotion does not have an adverse effect on others.

The ability to discriminate between appropriate and inappropriate expressions of emotions

The ability to discriminate between appropriate and inappropriate expressions of emotions involves drawing on the awareness of the wide range of possible behaviours resulting from emotions. It also involves the ability to determine which are appropriate expressions of these emotions, i.e. those that do not hurt anyone else either physically or emotionally or stop them from doing what they are wanting to do, and which are inappropriate expressions of these emotions i.e. that hurt others either physically or emotionally and/or stop them doing what they want to do.

An example

Reuben often feels lonely at playtimes. He has learnt that it is acceptable to feel lonely and want to do something about it. Reuben also knows that it is acceptable to express this emotion by telling other children that he feels lonely and asking if he can join in with their game. He also understands that it is not acceptable to run up to a child and hit them because they have not asked him to join in their game. Therefore Reuben is developing the ability to discriminate between appropriate and inappropriate expressions of this emotion.

An understanding of the role of emotions in learning

An understanding of the role of emotions in learning involves an appreciation that emotions affect performance. Emotions can affect performance either positively or negatively. To understand the effect of emotions on learning children need to be able to recognise their personal triggers to emotions.

An example

Erica feels very nervous about her Year 2 SATs as she is very keen to do well. When Erica gets nervous she forgets what she has learnt and then starts to cry because she cannot complete the task. Erica recognises that the SATs tests are a trigger to her feeling nervous and that this has a negative effect on her performance. In order to try and manage this emotion Erica may discuss her feeling of nervousness with her teacher and ask for some help. Discussions during whole class Circle Time may also have given Erica some ideas about how other children in her class cope with feeling nervous.

The ability to manage the feelings of anger, fear, worry, loneliness, frustration and grief in an appropriate way

The ability to manage feelings, especially those that may lead to us feeling vulnerable such as anger, fear, worry, loneliness, frustration and grief, in an appropriate way involves being able to recognise and label these emotions. It may also involve an appreciation of triggers leading to these emotions. Once a feeling has been identified the knowledge of a range of strategies allowing for the appropriate management of this emotion should be available for use. The range of appropriate strategies will vary from emotion to emotion, person to person and situation to situation.

An example

Lee often feels frustrated when he is not chosen for the football team and given a place as a substitute instead. Lee recognises this emotion in himself and understands the link between his position in the football team and the feeling of frustration. Lee has developed a way of managing this emotion so that it does not result in difficulties between him and his manager. He gently warms up throughout the match indicating that he is keen to play, taking his mind off the fact that he is not playing and removing him from close proximity to anyone with whom he may take out his frustration.

The ability to manage a variety of emotional states through the use of relaxation and calming techniques and visualisation

The ability to manage a variety of emotional states, through the use of relaxation and calming techniques and visualisation, involves being able to recognise a range of emotions and appreciate the need to manage these. There also needs to be an appreciation that when experiencing strong emotions there is a higher level of arousal. Relaxation and calming techniques can be used to lower these levels of arousal as can visualisation.

An example
Daniel feels very angry when he gets told off by his teacher, especially if he feels that he is reprimanded for something that he has not done. Daniel understands that when he feels angry a range of physiological changes occur such as his heart beginning to beat faster, his hands becoming sweaty and his breathing becoming faster and shallower. When recognising these changes in himself Daniel has learned to concentrate on breathing rhythmically and when necessary he is able to visualise a time when he has felt relaxed and calm. This helps Daniel to manage his feelings of anger.

The ability to re-frame situations in a more positive way
The ability to re-frame situations in a more positive way involves the ability to understand that situations can be viewed in a variety of ways, some of which are helpful and some of which are unhelpful. Developing the ability to view situations in a positive way is helpful in managing emotions and in maintaining a sense of emotional wellbeing. This will also help to build resilience.

An example
Bushra is upset because she thought that the teacher was not listening to her when she was trying to explain why she had not done her homework. If Bushra views this situation in an unhelpful way she may think that the teacher does not care, that the teacher does not believe what she is saying or that the teacher is treating her unfairly. When re-framing the situation to view it in a more positive light Bushra may think that the teacher is busy and will listen to her later, that the teacher has not heard her or that she is not explaining herself clearly. When Bushra is able to view the situation in a positive way she is managing her emotions and in doing so prevents the situation from escalating further.

The ability to manage the feelings of rejection, guilt, jealousy and anger in an appropriate way
The ability to manage more complex feelings, especially those that may lead to us feeling vulnerable such as rejection, guilt, jealousy and anger in an appropriate way involves being able to recognise and label these emotions. It may also involve an appreciation of triggers leading to these emotions. Once a feeling has been identified the knowledge of a range of strategies, allowing for the appropriate management of this emotion, should be available for use. The range of appropriate strategies will vary from emotion to emotion, person to person and situation to situation.

An example
Charles feels jealous when he is not invited to tea with his friends. He is able to recognise and label this emotion and choose a strategy to manage this is an appropriate way. He may choose to re-frame this situation, to use some relaxation/calming techniques, to visualise a time when he has felt secure and loved or talk to his friend and confront his feelings in the situation.

The ability to use feelings in a positive way

The ability to use feelings in a positive way involves combining all of the skills described above and practising them in order to promote feelings of wellbeing, trust and security for all involved. This should occur in all situations with people learning through their previous experiences, including those of failure.

Management and Regulation of Emotions

Nursery, Reception and Year 1

Objective 1: **To understand the difference between an emotion and an action.**

Suggested activities

Watch clips of cartoons, or study nursery rhymes, and ask the children to identify both the emotions and the actions of the characters. This may be recorded in a table using either words or pictures. The table may look like this:

Character	Emotion	Action
Humpty Dumpty	Upset	Cried
Little Miss Muffet	Scared	Screamed and ran away

This table could be an interactive and ongoing display with children adding to it as and when appropriate. The teacher could provide envelopes containing cards that depict a range of emotions and actions so that the children can select them to suit the character and stick them on the chart.

During Circle Time sessions the focus may be to discuss situations that have arisen during playtimes. While discussing these situations there should be a clear distinction between the emotion of the child and the resulting action.

Children could be given picture or word cards, some of which relate to an emotion (Appendix 14, pp.112–113) (for example, happy, sad, scared) and some of which relate to an action (Appendix 15, pp.114–115) (for example, laughing, hitting, crying, running away). The children could then be asked to sort these into two groups (emotions and actions). The children may need this task to be mediated by the teacher due to the literacy demands of reading the cards.

Management and Regulation of Emotions

Year 2

Objective 1: **Recognising the range of possible reactions to a variety of emotions and the subsequent need to manage our emotions.**

Suggested activities

The children could be asked to think about the most appropriate behavioural responses to a variety of emotions. For example, they could be asked, 'If you were feeling very angry what is the best thing that you could do?' The reply may be to count to ten, walk away or tell a teacher or my mum. This activity could be continued by then asking the children to think about the most inappropriate behavioural responses to a variety of emotions. For example, they could be asked, 'If you were feeling very angry what is the worst thing that you could do?' The reply may be to hit, kick or yell. This range of responses could then be used to highlight the need to manage our emotions appropriately so that we remain in control of our own behaviour and our behaviours are socially acceptable.

The children could create mobiles or spider diagrams to show the range of possible reactions to a variety of emotions. Each group could be given a different emotion for this activity and these could then be shared at the end of the session with more reactions being added if necessary. The mobile or spider diagram may look like this:

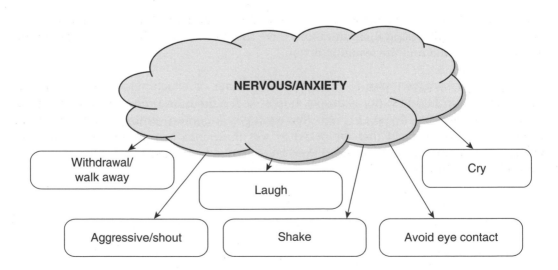

The children could be split into groups of two, three or four. All groups could then be given the same scenario (Appendix 16, p.116), for example, Fred was in class feeling bored. Each group could then be given a short period of time to develop a role play showing one way in which Fred may react in this situation. Each group could then perform their role play to the rest of the class with the teacher recording the range of reactions. Discussion could then centre around the range in the reactions to the same emotion. If this activity is repeated with other emotions/scenarios it is important that the teacher highlights the overlapping reactions. For example, if someone walks away it may be because they are angry, or scared, or nervous or bored or upset.

Objective 2: **Developing the ability to discriminate between acceptable and unacceptable expressions of emotions.**

Suggested activities

All of the activities described in Objective 1 could be extended to encourage the children to discriminate between acceptable and unacceptable expressions of emotions. Emphasis should be placed on acceptable expressions being associated with those that do not hurt others either physically or emotionally.

Children could be provided with action cards (Appendix 17, p.117) containing a range of reactions that may be associated with different emotions (for example: screaming, crying, walking away, hitting, laughing, singing, smiling, jumping up and down, yawning and kicking). They could then sort these into acceptable and unacceptable actions. Discussion could then follow regarding why they have sorted them as they have.

Children could watch cartoon clips and discuss whether the emotional reactions of the characters are acceptable or not. This activity could be extended so that the children (either individually, in small groups or as a whole class) write a letter to the cartoon production company suggesting that it would be better for the characters to express their emotions in a more acceptable manner. The children could provide examples of what this may include.

Objective 3: **Encouraging children to reflect on their own strategies for managing their emotions.**

Suggested activities

Class discussions could encourage children to reflect on their own strategies for managing their own emotions. Much of this work could be covered during Circle Time using activities such as:

- Sentence completion: 'When I feel lonely, I… (ask someone to play with me, go to the teacher, kick someone for not playing with me)'.

- Silent statements: 'If you have ever hit someone because you have felt angry stand up and swap places.' Those children that do swap places could be encouraged to think of more acceptable strategies for managing their feelings of anger, whilst those who do not swap places could be asked to reflect on what they do instead.

- Discussion during Circle Time could focus on the identification of more helpful/ acceptable strategies to use in order to manage emotions. For example, the children could be asked, 'What is a better way of dealing with your feeling of loneliness other than crying?'

- Children could discuss how the strategy that they have chosen to use to manage their emotion affects other people. For example, if a child's chosen strategy for dealing with excitement is to run around, screaming and jumping, they may realise that the effect that this has on those around them is to make them feel annoyed and jealous. The children could then be encouraged to reflect on whether this is what they are wanting to achieve.

There could be a class 'star of the week' given to the child who has expressed their emotions in an acceptable manner. Within the classroom there could be a box into which the children could post their reflections of a particular strategy they have used effectively to manage an emotion. At the end of the week the teacher could pick out an entry to receive the award or if there are only a small number in the box the children could vote.

The children could be encouraged to keep a log (Appendix 18, p.118) of their emotions along with the way that they managed the emotion and a way that they could improve on this next time. For example, the log may look like this:

Date	Trigger	Emotion	Strategy	Improvement
22 May	My birthday	Happy	Singing at the top of my voice	Keep my feelings of happiness inside and concentrate on my work in class and sing at the top of my voice/talk to my friends at playtime

Management and Regulation of Emotions

Year 3

Objective 1: Understand the three stages associated with emotions and relate this to their own experience.

Suggested activities

The children should be introduced to a three staged approach to help them understand emotions. The three stages are:

- a trigger stage

- a thoughts stage

- an action stage.

The children could be encouraged to create their own class visual representation of the stages by means of a model. For example, the idea of a kettle could be used to represent the three stages of anger, with the trigger stage being represented by the plug, the thoughts stage being represented by the cord and the action or behavioural stage being represented by the water boiling inside the kettle and the steam escaping from the kettle.

Children should be given another opportunity to consider their own individual triggers to emotions. Refer to activities outlined in the self-awareness strand for Year 1 (Objective 3, p.17) in Chapter Three for further ideas. The children could record their triggers, either using a table, mind map or pictures.

Children should be given the opportunity to discuss thoughts that might be associated with the triggers to their emotions. This may be achieved by asking children to recall situations in which a particular emotion has been experienced and consider the range of thoughts they may have had relating to the trigger. For example, Paul felt angry when his brother stood on his remote control car. He may have thought 'he's done it on purpose' or 'it was an accident and he didn't mean to' or 'I shouldn't have left it on the floor'. Different ways of doing this may be to use Circle Time, situation cards (Appendix 4, p.100) or role play.

Children should be given the opportunity to discuss the actions that might be associated with their emotions. This will be an extension of the work done in Years 1 (Objective 1, p.57) and Year 2 (Objectives 1 and 2, pp.58–59). At this stage the children should be able to relate specific emotions and actions from their own experiences.

The children should then be encouraged to combine their understanding of triggers, thoughts and actions to specific emotions or situations. They should demonstrate this understanding by recording events from their own experience in the form of a table (Appendix 19, p.119). For example:

Trigger	Emotion(s)	Thought	Action
My dog died	Grief, sadness or relief	He was ill and in pain	Cry

Objective 2: **Developing a range of strategies to help us to manage our emotions appropriately.**

Children should be taught a variety of strategies for managing their emotions. Before they can do this they must recognise that emotions can be problematic and want to learn how to manage them more effectively. A number of the strategies outlined below would be appropriate for managing different emotions, for example, anger, anxiety, fear, loneliness and excitement.

Suggested activities

Acknowledging emotion
Children need to be able to identify the emotion that they are experiencing before they are able to begin using strategies to manage the emotion. In order for these strategies to be effective they should be used at the earliest possible stage. Therefore it is important that the children are able to identify their own personal early warning signs.

A range of activities for developing the ability to recognise emotions in oneself are outlined in the self-awareness strand (Chapter Three).

Sharing emotions with others
After acknowledging an emotion, children should be encouraged to share the emotion they are experiencing with somebody else. This could be an adult or another child. By sharing the way that they are feeling children are engaging in the process of accepting the way that they feel. Through discussion with other people an appropriate way of managing the emotion can be established. Initially the teacher may need to direct discussion as a mediator and may draw on the strategies below to do so. This activity could be used at an individual level as and when incidents occur or during whole class sessions such as Circle Time.

Another activity could be to work out scripts that could be useful for managing certain emotions in context. For example, if a child sulks on the playground because she has nobody to play with, a useful, predetermined script may be 'I'm feeling lonely, please can I join in with your game?'. The scripts for a range of emotions could be made into posters and displayed around the classroom.

Avoiding triggers

Children will have already completed work requiring them to identify triggers to their various emotions. Children should recap on their own personal triggers to an emotion and underline those that could be avoided. For example, if the children were focusing on the emotion of frustration, Mary's triggers may include:

- being told to do something
- not being able to do my work
- being shouted at
- too much noise to concentrate
- not being listened to
- sitting next to Fred in maths
- tidying my bedroom when it is a mess
- not being allowed to watch my choice of TV programme.

Mary underlined those listed above because she thought that she could avoid them. For example, she could ask to sit by another child in maths, she could keep her bedroom more tidy so that she did not have to spend a long time tidying it up and ask for help so that she was able to do her work.

This activity can be repeated with a variety of emotions and the children should be encouraged to apply this knowledge to their lives. Their attempts to do this could be discussed during Circle Time and any successes shared with the rest of the class. In doing this the children may learn from, and be motivated by, their peers.

Positive self-talk

Positive self-talk involves the children using an internal monologue, developed by themselves, to overcome negative emotions controlling their behaviour. This will also provide the child with a distraction from the trigger that is causing the emotion.

Initially a single word is chosen by the child. This word should provide an association with calming down and relaxing for the child, for example: cool, calm or chill. When a child recognises that they are beginning to experience a strong emotion that may impact upon them in a negative way they should be encouraged to repeat their target word.

As the children become familiar with the use of positive self-talk they can be encouraged to develop a positive sentence to repeat when they feel that their emotions are impacting upon them negatively. Such a sentence may include, 'I can do this.'

Children could share their experiences of using this strategy during Circle Time. The use of role play may enable children to use the strategy with more confidence.

Stop-think-go framework

This strategy requires that, when the children first become aware of an emotion impacting upon them negatively, their first response is to stop. This then allows them time to think about the situation and how they might respond best to it. The final stage of this approach is for the children to carry out the course of action that they consider to be the most positive. This technique prompts relaxation, resisting impulsivity and not dwelling on unhelpful negative thoughts.

This framework can be represented visually by the use of a poster depicting a set of traffic lights, with red indicating stop, amber indicating think and green indicating go. Placing the poster in a prominent position will encourage the children to use it. The strategy needs to be taught so that children have a variety of positive options open to them at the thinking stage. These may include:

- walking away

- asking a teacher/adult for help

- not answering back

- using positive self-talk

- explaining to the other child/adult how they are making you feel.

The children could each make their own bookmark with traffic lights on. They could annotate these so that they have a range of strategies available to them that they feel comfortable using.

The children could be given opportunities to act out trigger situations. While some children are acting out a scenario another child, or initially the teacher, could provide a commentary on what the target child is doing, i.e. when they have stopped, asking them what strategies they are considering, and then which positive strategy they are choosing to use. Practicing this in a safe, structured environment may allow for generalisation of the strategy.

Anchoring

This is a technique taken from neuro-linguistic programming. It describes the process by which memory recall becomes associated with (anchored to) a stimulus, such as touch, word or sight. The perception of the stimulus (the anchor) leads by reflex to the anchored response occurring.

Basic anchoring involves:

Step 1 – thinking of a time when the child experienced a strong positive emotion, opposite to the one that needs to be managed. For example, to manage feelings of anxiety the child remembers a time of feeling relaxed, e.g. watching a cartoon.

Step 2 – Recalling the desired emotion by using an action such as pushing together the thumb and middle finger. This action should then trigger the previous positive emotion (in this case of feeling relaxed). The negative emotion should then be minimised.

Breathing techniques

Children can be taught to control their breathing as a way of helping them to relax. This technique should be used at the earliest opportunity if it is to be successful. Two breathing techniques are listed below:

Square breathing

The children are taught to focus on a four-sided object (for example, a book, a whiteboard, a poster) and while tracking the sides of the object with their eyes they breathe around the four sides, as shown below:

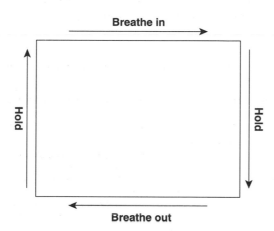

This pattern of breathing should be repeated until the child feels calm and relaxed.

Deep breathing

The children are taught to concentrate on breathing deeply in through the nose, holding, then slowly releasing the breath through the mouth. By concentrating on regular breathing in this way they calm the body and stop focusing on the trigger and the emotion that they are unable to manage.

Buddy system

This strategy could be used to support children who are developing skills to manage a particular emotion. The teacher should be responsible for pairing a child who has difficulty managing an emotion with one who is able to do this successfully. Depending on circumstances this could be a child who is in the same class or possibly an older child. The teacher should set aside time to allow the pairs to meet and may act as a facilitator during the discussions. If a pair of children cannot decide on appropriate ways to manage emotions or particular situations then a box could be available to post the situation in and this could be emptied regularly with class discussions generating appropriate ways to address the issue. For example, if during a discussion between the two buddies one felt sad because his mum and dad had just split up and he was getting into trouble for lack of concentration the problem could be posted anonymously. The class and the teacher could then make suggestions of how to manage the situation better. Possible suggestions may include giving the child the opportunity to talk to someone else who has been through the same experience; talking to teacher at the beginning of each day to 'offload'; the buddy to gently remind the child to refocus on the class activity.

Objective 3: **Developing an understanding that some emotions can be used in either a positive or negative way.**

Suggested activities

Children could sort responses to particular emotions into those responses that are helpful or unhelpful. This could be done by using clips from films, cartoons or television or characters from stories.

Children could list ways in which they use some emotions negatively or positively.

An example of this, using 'frustration', is shown in the table below:

Positive response	Negative response
Drive to succeed at a task	Prevents completion of a task
Warn others	Impeded concentration

Responses from the children's lists could be discussed and displayed on the wall and added to accordingly.

Management and Regulation of Emotions

Year 4

Objective 1: **Development of relaxation techniques which can be used to manage a variety of emotional states.**

Suggested activities

Children should be taught a variety of strategies for managing their emotions. Before they can do so they must recognise that emotions can be problematic and want to learn how to manage them more effectively. A number of the strategies outlined below would be appropriate for managing different emotions e.g.: anger, anxiety, fear, loneliness and excitement.

Muscle tensing and relaxing

Children should be able to recognise when their body is relaxed and when it is tense so as to identify when feelings are affecting their bodies. In order to do this they may practice tensing their muscles. The teacher should lead this activity and encourage the children to start tensing their muscles beginning with their feet and then moving to their calves, thighs, buttocks, stomach, chest, arms, hands, neck and face. Once the whole body is tense the teacher then asks the children to release the tension in reverse order. The children could then discuss what it felt like when they were tense and when they were relaxed.

Children could work in pairs and be encouraged to relax all of their muscles so that they feel like a 'rag doll.' Their partner could then test how relaxed they are by lifting an arm, then a leg and seeing whether it flops back down, which would indicate they are relaxed.

Once children are able to relax their muscles consciously they could be encouraged to use this as a way of regulating their emotional state. In doing this their attention will once again be diverted from the trigger that is causing a problem.

Breathing

It may be necessary to repeat the suggested activities aimed at developing square breathing and deep breathing that are outlined in Year 3, Objective 2 (pp.62–65). As an extension of this, children could now be encouraged to develop their own way of breathing as a relaxation technique. This may incorporate some visual cues to help the child focus. An example may be for a football fan to visualise a football pitch and focus on breathing around the perimeter of the pitch. Another example may be to focus on a pendulum movement of a clock and breathe rhythmically to that.

Physical exercise

Some children may find that physical exercise helps them to manage their emotional state by providing a release and a distraction. Such activities may include going for a short walk, e.g. on an errand or doing exercises in the classroom such as 'head, shoulders, knees and toes'.

Objective 2: **Development of visualisation used to manage a variety of emotional states.**

Suggested activities

Visualisation

- The teacher should ensure that the children are in a relaxed, comfortable position with their eyes closed. The teacher then reads a script to the class, encouraging them to imagine themselves there. The script needs to focus on a place that is generally considered to be relaxing. An example of a script is:

'It is a warm sunny day and you are walking under some trees beside a small gurgling stream. You lie down on a soft patch of grass right beside the stream and gently put your hand into the warm water. You feel the water trickling between your fingers and the sun warming your face. You can hear the birds chirping above you in the trees and when you look up the sun is making patterns through the leaves. As you lie there feeling warm and content you relax your breathing and slowly drift off to sleep.'

This script should be followed by a short period of silence that can be used for personal reflection. The teacher should then gently bring the children back to the present. A script, such as the one below could be used for this purpose.

'Now I want you to open your eyes slowly and look around you at the room. You are back in the classroom. Now sit up slowly and take several deep breaths'.

- An extension of this activity would be for the children to write their own scripts.

- Children may be taught to think of a place and time where they felt relaxed, such as in bed, on a beach, having their hair brushed. Recalling this event, visualising themselves there and their feelings of relaxation at the time, can induce similar feelings when the child feels the need to manage the feelings that they are experiencing. If it is helpful the scene can be visualised as happening within a real or imaginary hoop placed in front of them. The child only has to step inside the hoop to bring to mind the feeling of relaxation associated with that place. Children who have difficulty could use a photograph or painting of the place as a concrete reminder.

Objective 3: **Developing the ability to apply the relaxation/calming techniques outlined above.**

Suggested activities

- The teacher should provide opportunities for the children to practise the strategies listed above. This would be particularly useful at stressful times, for example, after playtime, lunchtime, exams or tests, etc. These strategies should be practised as regularly as possible, perhaps at the beginning or end of Circle Time sessions.

- The children could use a diary or chart to record their own personal use of any relaxation techniques. After using any technique the children should be encouraged to evaluate how useful that technique was in managing the emotion.

Management and Regulation of Emotions

Year 5

Objective 1: **Developing the ability to re-frame situations in a more positive way.**

Re-framing is a technique used to help people think about difficult situations or events in a more positive way than they otherwise would. The following table highlights the desirable shift in thinking that can be achieved by teaching the technique of re-framing.

Situation/event	Initial thoughts	Re-framed thoughts
Someone knocks your arm when you are writing in class	• He did that on purpose to spoil my work • He is always picking on me • He wanted to get me into trouble	• He was just reaching to get the rubber and accidentally knocked my arm • Somebody else pushed him and he knocked my arm
You are trying to watch your favourite TV programme and your sister turns it over	• I'm never allowed to watch my programmes • She's always being unkind to me • She knows that is my favourite programme	• She didn't realise that I was watching it • I watched my programme last week and so it is her turn this week

Suggested activities

• Provide the children with ambiguous pictures or scenarios (Appendix 20, p.120) and ask them to think of as many alternative interpretations for that scene/scenario as possible. This will develop the children's ability to view situations in different ways. The children could then sort their list of interpretations into positive/helpful thoughts and negative/unhelpful thoughts.

• The children should be encouraged to brainstorm situations where re-framing may be useful in their everyday lives. This will enable them to see when the technique may be usefully applied.

• The children should be given regular opportunities to practice re-framing situations/ events using role play and discussion.

• When reading books the children could be encouraged to view situations experienced by a fictional character in a number of different ways.

Objective 2: **Developing an understanding of the emotion of grief.**

Developing an understanding of grief is one way in which children can begin to manage this emotion. The children should be taught about the stages of grief which are outlined below, with emphasis being placed on understanding that all of these emotions are normal:

- Shock – This is often the first response and may take the form of physical pain or numbness. More often people may experience a feeling of abnormal calm.

- Denial – This is another common response to a bereavement and involves someone behaving as if the person/animal is still alive.

- Sadness – Feelings of denial may begin to change with sadness/emptiness becoming the most dominant emotion. This may be accompanied by emotional releases such as crying which eases the pain.

- Guilt – Feelings of guilt may be experienced which may be associated with real or imagined negative events/actions. This is associated with feeling a need to take responsibility for what has happened.

- Anxiety – Feelings of anxiety are likely to be experienced when a loss is accepted. When the loss is accepted people often begin to feel anxious about possible changes and loneliness. This anxiety may lead to panic.

- Aggression and Anger – Feelings of anger are often directed towards individuals who were unable to prevent the loss e.g. doctor or family members. Feelings of anger may also be directed towards the dead person/animal for the pain and upheaval that their death has caused.

Suggested activity
The children could discuss a story read by the teacher (such as Badger's *Parting Gift*, Varley, S., 1994) and discuss the feelings of the characters left behind. They could use the stages outlined above to help them do this. They could also discuss how they feel listening to the story.

Objective 3: **Developing ways of managing grief in ourselves and in others.**

Suggested activities
Children could be encouraged to look at ways of remembering people/pets positively. This could be achieved by looking at how famous people have been remembered and at how members of the children's families have been remembered.

During Circle Time the children could discuss appropriate responses to grief in others. These may include:

- Acknowledging it.

- Talking about it.

- Sensitivity.

Children should be provided with opportunities to practise these skills within a safe environment, for example during role play or Circle Time. It may be appropriate to hold a class remembrance for a pet that has recently died, as then the children can give expression to feelings of grief and practice talking to people about it.

If a well-known figure dies then this should provide an opportunity for the children to discuss loss and bereavement and consider how it makes them feel.

The children could watch clips of videos such as the death of Aslan in *The Lion, the Witch and the Wardrobe* and discuss their responses to the scene.

Objective 4: **Recognising the importance of adjusting one's own levels of emotion in view of the emotional state of others.**

Suggested activity

- The children could view video or TV clips as an introduction to understanding how one person adjusts the expression of their emotions because of the emotional state of the other. When they have watched a clip the children could be asked to identify the emotion of one of the characters and then identify how the other person may have adjusted the expression of their emotion.

- During Circle Time children could discuss real situations where they have adjusted their own expression of an emotion in light of another's emotion.

Management and Regulation of Emotions

Year 6

***Objective 1*: To develop further and use new and familiar strategies to help us to manage our emotions appropriately.**

At this stage the children should be familiar with a range of strategies for managing their emotions. These are listed below and references for details relating to each strategy are given in brackets.

- Identifying the triggers to their emotions (Management and Regulation of Emotions; Year 3, Objective 2, p.63).

- Sharing emotions with others in order to clarify how we are feeling and try to develop an appropriate way of managing the emotion with the help of another (Management and Regulation of Emotions; Year 3, Objective 2, pp.65–66).

- Positive self-talk (Management and Regulation of Emotions; Year 3, Objective 2, p.63).

- Breathing techniques (Management and Regulation of Emotions; Year 3, Objective 2, p.65 and Year 4, Objective 1, p.67).

- Stop-think-go framework (Management and Regulation of Emotions; Year 3, Objective 2, p.64).

- Anchoring (Management and Regulation of Emotions; Year 3, Objective 2, p.64).

- Buddy system (Management and Regulation of Emotions; Year 3, Objective 2, pp.65–66).

- Relaxation techniques (Management and Regulation of Emotions; Year 4, Objective 1, p.67).

- Visualisation techniques (Management and Regulation of Emotions; Year 4, Objective 2, p.68).

- Re-framing (Management and Regulation of Emotions; Year 5, Objective 1, p.70).

As the children have already been introduced to the above strategies for managing their emotions, a re-cap of the above may be sufficient and the children should be encouraged to apply these strategies to a wider range of emotions. The following strategies may be appropriate to teach to Year 6 children in order to equip them with further strategies for managing their emotions.

Suggested activities

Distraction techniques
The children could be encouraged to develop their own personal distraction techniques. These may include reciting words to their favourite songs, counting (forwards, backwards or in multiples) or imagining themselves experiencing an enjoyable/relaxing time. All of the above distraction techniques need to be done silently in their head and no-one else should be aware that this technique is being used.

Developing an emotion management plan
This could be viewed as an extension of the stop-think-go framework. The children should be encouraged to develop their own staged plan that can be used to manage a variety of emotions that may be problematic for them. This plan may incorporate any of the strategies listed above but should not contain too many steps. This plan must be something that works for the child and should be practiced/reviewed frequently with changes being made if an element of the plan is not effective. Eventually this plan should be internalised and provide an automatic response to problematic emotions.

An emotion management plan may look something like this:

- **Recognise** that my emotional state has changed and identify the emotion that I am now experiencing.

- **Appreciate** that this emotion, if expressed in a certain way, can be problematic for me and those around me.

- **Distract** myself from the emotion that I am experiencing and the trigger that lead to it, by using breathing and visualisation techniques.

Or

- Note change of emotional state

- Breathe regularly and rhythmically while dropping my shoulders

- Refocus on the task.

Share currently used ways of managing emotions
By the time the children have reached Year 6 and have been taught about emotions over a period of years they are likely to have developed their own strategies for managing their emotions as well as those that have been explicitly taught. Consequently, it may be useful, during Circle Time, to build opportunities for children to share strategies that they have found useful. This will allow children to widen their repertoire of strategies for managing their emotions.

6
Relationships

The ability to establish and maintain relationships with others involves an awareness of one's own emotional state in relation to the emotional state of another. In order to develop fulfilling reciprocal relationships children will need to draw on all of the emotional competencies already covered; self-awareness, understanding and recognising emotion in others and management and regulation of their own emotions. In addition to these three emotional competencies, children need to develop a set of social skills (such as those involved in turn taking, sharing, resolving conflicts, negotiating, etc.) that will enable them to establish and maintain relationships with others. The association between these three competencies, social skills and the development of relationships can be seen below:

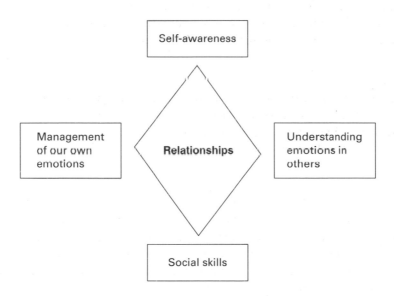

A suggested progression of the competencies involved in developing relationships is outlined below. They include abilities in:

- o Transition from adult-child relationship to playing alongside and with peers.
- o Developing turn taking skills.

- Developing the ability to share.
- Developing co-operative play skills.
- Developing an understanding and appreciation of friendships.
- Developing the skills required for successful group work.
- Recognising individual strengths and weaknesses.
- Developing the skills associated with successful conflict resolution.
- Developing an understanding of discrimination and equality, focusing on racism/sexism/disability.
- Developing the skills associated with successful negotiation.

Each of these competencies will now be considered individually and examples are given of children demonstrating the skill. It is important to remember that because children learn from 'significant others' you as the teacher will be modelling the competencies for the children. Explicit modelling of these skills, including describing what you are doing or have done, will be beneficial for the children.

The transition from adult-child relationship to playing alongside and with peers

In order for children to extend their relationships so that they include other children of a similar age, they need to be able to tolerate other children playing in their 'space'. The next step is likely to involve children responding in a positive manner to approaches from other children, they may then go on to initiate such interactions themselves. This will involve children accepting that they are not always able to have an adult's undivided attention and that they are members of a group, other than a family group. This also requires children to feel secure enough to separate from their main caregivers. Many children will have already developed these skills prior to beginning in a Reception class.

An example

Benjamin enters Nursery with his mother who helps him hang up his coat and gives him a goodbye kiss and leaves as he walks towards his favourite activity – the sand. Benjamin then happily allows other children to play in the sand near him and he approaches another child to show him what he is doing.

Developing turn taking skills

In order for children to develop turn taking skills they need to be able to accommodate the needs of another person as well as their own needs. This requires a less self-centred approach to interaction. Many children require practice in the skill of turn taking and should learn this skill initially with just one other adult before extending it to include one child and then an increasing number of children.

An example

Fiona is playing on the computer in class and another child is standing beside her. Fiona acknowledges the presence of the person and offers her a turn on the computer. When the child has had two turns on the computer Fiona asks for another turn. This indicates that

Fiona has developed an understanding of the concept of turn taking that she is able to apply to her interactions with her peers.

Developing the ability to share

The ability to share involves an understanding of a mutual benefit in the relationship and an appreciation that it requires 'give and take'. A child capable of sharing spontaneously, without prompting from an adult, would recognise the needs of the other person and adjust their behaviour to include them. Sharing may involve objects but the emphasis is on the relationship and therefore children may share imaginative games, special times, secrets and stories, etc. The children need to be confident enough in themselves to please another.

An example

John has a packet of crisps and spontaneously offers to share them with his friend Paul. Paul says thank you, sits beside John and they chat happily as they share the crisps.

Developing co-operative play skills

Co-operative play skills involve combining the individual skills of playing or interacting with other children, turn taking and sharing.

An example

Vaj and his friends dress up as doctors, nurses and patients while playing in the role play corner in the classroom. They smile, laugh and play happily together, thus sharing the enjoyment of the game. At the same time they also share the dressing up clothes and equipment so that everyone has something to wear and play with.

Developing an understanding and appreciation of friendships

Developing an understanding and appreciation of friendships involves recognising the qualities of a friend. These qualities include loyalty, respect, reliability, trust, caring, openness, honesty and having shared interests.

An example

Pauline asks Jill to, 'Come and build a Lego house with me'. Jill replies, 'Yes, good idea, then we can put the puppy in the dog bed in the kitchen'.

Developing the skills required for successful group work

Successful group work requires the skills of effective communication, listening skills, turn taking and concentration on the task. It also needs some understanding that working together as a team may increase the likelihood of achieving a goal that might not have been possible for one person to attain alone. Different perspectives and roles provided by the individuals give a breadth of experience to the group and allow the individuals to use their strengths for the benefit of everyone. The emphasis should be on teamwork and co-operation rather than competition.

An example
Children were studying the Ancient Egyptians in history and following a class discussion on the importance of the River Nile they were split into groups of three and asked to find out more about the different ways in which it was important. As one of the children in the group was very good at using the computer the group decided that they should look up information on the internet, while another child who was good at reading looked up information in books. The third child, who was good at drawing, copied a map of the River Nile out of a book, so that the group could record their information in this format. By combining the strengths of each group member and engaging in an initial process of deciding on what role each group member should take (involving speaking, listening and turn talking skills), the group were able to complete the task to a better standard than any of them would have been capable of achieving individually.

Recognising individual strengths and weaknesses
Recognising individual strengths and weaknesses involves the ability to identify the difference between a strength and a weakness, i.e. something that you or someone else does well as opposed to something you or someone else finds difficult.

An example
Laura, Nathan and Sophie were asked to discuss and record a range of ideas for writing a story about a fire. Nathan provided lots of very creative ideas for which Laura and Sophie praised him, as they recognised that this was his strength. Laura and Sophie were also able to recognise that writing was a particular weakness for Nathan and therefore they supported him during this part of the task.

Developing an awareness of conflict situations and how these can be resolved
Developing an awareness of conflict situations involves the ability to recognise a difficult situation and realise that steps need to be taken in order to ameliorate it. In order to achieve this, children will need to identify situations within their own lives which give rise to conflict and develop an understanding of how they currently tackle these situations. Children then need to be able to distinguish between positive and negative responses to conflict situations and begin to choose the positive strategies over the negative strategies.

An example
Tommy was told to do his homework by his dad but wanted to go and play on his bike instead. On a previous occasion, Tommy has responded to this request by shouting at his dad and running off upstairs. Tommy was now able to recognise that this was a conflict situation and so he tried to think of a positive strategy for dealing with it. On this occasion he tried to talk to his dad and persuade him that it would be dark by 5.00pm and that he would do his homework as soon as he came in. This was successful and resulted in the conflict being resolved.

Developing an understanding of discrimination and equality, focusing on racism and disability

In order to develop an understanding of discrimination and equality children need to begin to value differences in people. They may begin to do this by looking at different races and disabilities and learning more about these. This may then allow them to begin to appreciate that their lack of understanding leads to discrimination. In order to address issues of discrimination, work needs to focus on changing their own attitudes and beliefs.

An example

Emily has epilepsy that has proved difficult to control and so results in frequent fits at school. As a consequence a number of her peers are frightened of her as they do not want to be near her when she has a fit. Discussions about this with the teacher helps those children to realise that the reason for them not viewing her as an equal class member is that they are frightened and do not understand what is happening. Following this discussion the teacher worked with the class, to develop a better understanding of epilepsy. After this work the children were no longer afraid to be near Emily, felt more comfortable around her and began to build a positive relationship with her. Once they started to do this they began to view Emily as a child with similar interests to everyone else in the class, rather than as the 'child with epilepsy'. By addressing the issue directly barriers were successfully broken down.

Developing the skills associated with successful negotiation

Successful negotiation involves an appreciation that this is the best way to resolve conflict situations as well as being a tool that is useful in persuasion and communication in general. Negotiation involves understanding that successful outcomes generally result in all parties feeling positive and that this will often involve an element of compromise. Negotiation is a process reliant on the ability to empathise with another person(s). It is a structured process involving; identifying what you want, identifying what the other person wants, generating a range of possible solutions and ensuring that the solution chosen benefits all involved to some extent. In order to engage in this process, children will need well developed speaking and listening skills and a willingness to compromise. It is likely that children will need to practice these skills when interacting with an adult before applying them to their everyday interactions with their peers.

An example

Sarah and Sylvia both wanted to sit at the same desk in class and realised that this was not possible. Sarah explained that she wanted to sit in that seat because otherwise she could not see the board as her glasses were being mended. Sylvia wanted to sit there because she wanted to sit next to her best friend. When the girls tried to think of possible solutions to this problem they thought of; moving Sylvia's friend to another table so that they could sit together, Sarah only sitting at that desk for lessons where she needed to be able to see the board, Sarah sitting there until her glasses were mended and then swapping back or that neither of them sit in that seat. The girls decided that Sarah could sit there when she needed to see the board and that Sylvia sat there for all other lessons. It was also decided that when Sarah's glasses were mended they would go back to their original seats.

Relationships

Nursery and Reception

Objective 1: To nurture the transition from adult–child relationship to playing with and alongside others.

Suggested activities

To encourage a child to separate willingly from their parent or carer:

- Children who are reluctant to separate from their parent or carer should be guided to a favourite activity on arrival at Nursery or school. This should act as a distraction and ease the child into the Nursery setting. If necessary the child could be given a card with a visual reminder of the favourite activity by the parent before arriving at Nursery.

- Children should be encouraged to greet a reluctant child and activities should be designed that encourage the child to interact, and therefore develop new, positive relationships, with different adults.

- Children should be made aware of the order of activities within the setting; this can be done through the use of a visual timetable, which could be taken home so that the child can be reassured about what will be happening in Nursery or school.

To encourage children to play alongside other children:

- The teacher could set up the nursery or class so that small groups of children are directed to an activity, for example, the home corner. This will encourage children to play alongside the other children in their group.

- Children's awareness of other children could be raised through adult prompts and modelling. The attention of children who have not yet developed an awareness of others should be directed towards children who are engaged in an activity. This may be done by the teacher saying to the child, 'Have you seen what Bradley is doing?'. If the child does not respond, the teacher could provide a further prompt such as ' Bradley is floating a boat in the water, why don't we go and play in the water too?'. The teacher should guide the child towards the activity and initially encourage them to imitate the play of the other child.

To encourage children to play with each other:

- Children should be given the opportunity to engage in symbolic role play activities with their peers, for example, in the home corner.

- Children may benefit from the introduction of structured games or activities into unstructured times, for example, playtime, to encourage playing together. Initially this will need to be led by an adult who encourages children to participate in the game or activity.

- Teacher praise and rewards should be used as a way of recognising that children are playing together and to encourage them to repeat this behaviour.

Objective 2: **To develop the skills associated with turn taking.**

Suggested activities

- During small group or whole class speaking and listening activities the teacher could use an object to indicate whose turn it is. This object could be passed around the group and when a child has the object they can speak while the others listen. This provides a visual prompt as to whose turn it is. When children are used to this, the object or visual prompt should be removed and children encouraged to indicate whose turn it is next.

- Games that promote turn taking such as board games, I-spy or card games can be used to reinforce this skill, firstly in a small group led by an adult and then in larger groups before generalising this skill to free play situations.

- The class could brainstorm times when it is helpful to take turns and display this for reference in the form of either pictures or as a wall display. This will help the children to generalise and practice their turn taking skills.

Relationships

Year 1

Objective 1: **To develop the skills associated with sharing.**

Suggested activities
During Circle Time the children could discuss the concept of sharing using activities such as:

- Sentence completion: 'The last time I shared something was...(when I gave Adam some of my crisps at playtime)'. 'When I share I feel ...(kind)'. 'When someone shared their things with me I feel ... happy)'.

- Silent statements: 'If you have shared something with someone today swap places.' Those children that do swap places could be asked to describe their experience of sharing.

- Children could discuss how their behaviour (sharing or not sharing) may impact on their feelings and those of others.

The children could be asked to design posters that promote sharing, which could then be displayed around their classroom and throughout the school. The children could be encouraged to create slogans for their posters such as 'It's super to share'.

The teacher should try and spot children as they are in the process of sharing and provide immediate reinforcement of this behaviour, possibly using a previously agreed motto such as 'super sharing'.

Teachers could set up a 'super sharers' box in the classroom. This may be made from an old shoebox decorated by the children to make it significant to them. The names of children observed sharing should then be posted into this box. The teacher may wish to give a reward to the child whose name appears most frequently in the box that week. This process will initially need to be teacher-led, with children also being encouraged to post names into the box, in the hope that it will eventually be a child-led activity.

Objective 2: **To encourage co-operative play.**

Suggested activities

Children could be involved in teacher directed play activities where co-operation is required in order to play the game. Games could include pairs card games, bingo, lotto or role play (Appendix 21, p.121) with given roles for two or three people. Initially the teacher will need to allocate the roles within the group but as the children become more familiar with the processes involved in co-operative play they should be encouraged jointly to choose the roles themselves.

The teacher could facilitate whole class or small group discussions focusing on 'playing together'. During this discussion the emphasis should be placed on highlighting the range of skills that are required to achieve this, such as listening, turn taking, non-verbal language and sharing. These skills should be reinforced and practiced as frequently as possible, with visual reminders being created to remind the children of the skills involved in playing together. The displays may take a variety of forms, two of which are outlined below:

- Photographs of the children when they are engaged in a co-operative play activity could be taken and later discussed either as a whole class or small group. The children could then identify the range of skills that are being used in the photograph and use this information to create a display.

- A display (using a combination of words and pictures) in the form of an equation could be used to emphasise the skills needed to play together, for example:

| Playing together | = | Listening | + | Taking turns | + | Sharing |

Relationships

Year 2

Objective 1: **To develop an understanding of the concept of 'friendship'.**

Suggested activities

During Circle Time the children could discuss the concept of friendship using activities such as:

- Sentence completion: 'My friends are... I like it when my friends... (play with me) and My best friend is... because...'

- Silent statements: 'If you have played with a friend today swap places'. Those children that do swap places could be asked to describe what they have done with their friend.

- Children could discuss how having friends makes them feel and what it feels like to not have friends.

- Children could brainstorm the question 'What is a friend?'

Children could be asked to produce an annotated picture of their 'ideal friend'. They should then take turns to share this with the rest of the class so that key/core features of a good friend can be identified.

The children could each write sentences explaining why they are a good friend and put these into a box. During Circle Time the teacher could then read out a selection and the children should try to guess who it is!

A quiz game 'The Fantastic Friend Quiz' could be developed by the teacher and the class. During this quiz, three or four selected children will be asked a set of questions relating to friendship. These could be information questions or questions based on desirable actions in a given scenario. It is important that the questions asked are open-ended so that they do not have a right or wrong answer. The selected children would then answer verbally the questions asked with the rest of class then voting for the best answer. Some children may be chosen to justify why they voted for one answer rather than another. The quiz could be a weekly event with the winner being presented with a 'Fantastic Friend' certificate.

Objective 2: **How to deal with friendship fall-outs.**

Suggested activities

Children could be provided with scenarios in which two friends fall out. They could then develop a role play based on this scenario trying to think of an ending that results in them both remaining friends. The children could then present their role play to the rest of the class who could brainstorm other ways that the characters could have dealt with the situation. If a number of ways are elicited a class discussion may focus on which ones are the most effective.

The teacher could describe a situation in which Emo falls out with his friend. The children could then be asked to write a letter to Emo advising him on strategies that may restore his friendship. Instead of writing a letter the children could do this as a phone call and tape their response or produce a cartoon.

The class could focus on the importance of apologising, considering why this is important and when it is appropriate to apologise. Within the safe context of the classroom, perhaps during Circle Time, children could be given opportunities to practice saying sorry to others. When the teacher observes a child apologising appropriately this could be reinforced through praise or a sticker.

Relationships

Year 3

Objective 1: **Recognising individual strengths and weaknesses.**

Suggested activities

The children could be asked to create profiles outlining their strengths and weaknesses. They could list things that they are good at and things that they need help with (Appendix 22, p.122). For example:

Things that I am good at	Things that I need help with
Tidying up	Reading
Maths	Spelling
Football	Drawing

The children could then be asked to consider the strengths and weaknesses of a partner. They should then be encouraged to share their lists before deciding how they could use this knowledge to help each other. This information could then be shared with the whole class during a Circle Time activity. One of the purposes of this activity is to boost the self-esteem of the children as it aims to highlight that everyone has strengths that can be used to benefit everyone. This will also help to create a strong class ethos and encourage the class to work together as a team.

The teacher should also take account of the information provided by the children as it may be useful for grouping the children for particular activities. Children could be grouped according to similar strengths or could be grouped in order to complement each other's strengths and weaknesses.

It would be useful to repeat this activity on a termly basis when setting new class objectives. This information could provide the basis for a display within the classroom.

A variation on this activity could be used with groups of 6–8 children, chosen randomly so that they are not with their friends. Each child's name is put at the top of a sheet of paper and the papers are passed around the group for each child to note a strength of the target person. They then fold the piece of paper over so that their comment cannot be read by anyone else and pass it to the next person. When all have commented on the piece of paper it is returned to the person whose name is at the top. They are then able to read a list of positive comments that others think about them. This will help the children to recognise the strengths of others within their class and boost the self-esteem of the children when they read their own piece of paper.

Objective 2: **Developing the skills necessary for successful group work.**

Suggested activities

This work builds on that covered during Year 1 but shifts the focus from co-operative play skills to co-operative work skills. The children could be given weekly tasks, for half a term, that require them to work co-operatively. The objective of working together as a group needs to be made explicit to the children at the start. Activities may include:

- developing a simple board game for younger children

- planning a class party/outing

- planning a class assembly

- re-creating a famous painting from smaller pieces of the picture

- baking activities

- create a puppet show

- producing the cover of a newspaper.

Following each group activity the children should be asked to reflect on how they worked together as a group. They could be asked be identify three strengths and three weaknesses of the group. The groups could then share with the rest of the class one thing that went particularly well in their group and one thing that they found difficult. The rest of the class could then provide suggestions as to how the difficulty could be overcome next time.

After a period of working together co-operatively on a range of tasks the children could be asked to prepare and present a short video clip outlining what makes a good team.

Relationships

Year 4

Objective 1: **To raise awareness of possible ways of resolving conflicts.**

Suggested activities

Initially the children should be asked to brainstorm the concept of conflict. By the end of this activity the children should understand conflict to encompass both verbal and physical disagreements, ranging from minor disagreements between friends to international war. There should be an understanding that a disagreement involves opposing views.

The children should then be encouraged to brainstorm ways of dealing with conflicts and record these on pieces of card. At this stage both positive and negative ways of dealing with conflicts should be recorded. These may include: verbally expressing yourself clearly and calmly, hitting someone, ignoring someone, shouting, throwing things, listening to the other person's view or compromising (see Appendix 23, p. 123 for examples). These cards should be kept for later use.

The children should then be introduced to three possible outcomes of a conflict situation; win/win, win/lose, lose/lose. A win-win outcome involves both parties feeling that the situation has been resolved positively. This usually involves compromise. A win-lose outcome involves one party getting what they want with the result that the other party get nothing. A lose-lose outcome involves neither party getting what they want.

For example, Paul and Mary both want to watch different television programmes at the same time. An example of a win-win outcome would be that Paul watches his programme now as it is not repeated and Mary watches her programme on Sunday when it is repeated. This results in both Mary and Paul feeling happy because they can both watch their programme. An example of a win-lose outcome would be that Mary watches her programme and Paul watches nothing. An example of a lose-lose outcome would be that their Mum turns off the television because of their arguing, resulting in neither of them watching their programmes.

The children could then be asked to reflect on these three outcomes of a conflict during Circle Time. A sentence completion activity such as, 'the last time I was in a win-win situation was...' could be used to facilitate this process. This will encourage the children to relate their own previous experiences to their new knowledge of conflict resolution outcomes.

Once the children are familiar with, and understand, the win-win, win-lose, lose-lose outcomes of a conflict, they can sort the cards produced previously (or those in Appendix 23, p.123) into the three categories.

The children could then watch television or film clips and discuss outcomes of conflicts in terms of win/win, win/lose, lose/lose.

Objective 2: **To develop a range of conflict resolution strategies.**

Suggested activities

The children should be given the opportunity to brainstorm as many win/win ways of resolving a conflict as possible. These may include compromising, apologising and seeking help. Each strategy should then be discussed in more detail with children being given the opportunity to role play win/win outcomes in given conflict situations. Follow-up discussions could then focus on the resulting emotions. These could be compared to the emotions felt when lose-lose and win-lose outcomes are role played. The strategies that result in win-win outcomes could then form the basis of a display to act as a visual reminder to the children of how conflicts can, and should, be resolved.

A class mediation system could also be set up. Children could be identified and then trained as mediators and be made available to help others resolve conflicts within the class (Stacey and Robinson, 1997). Schrumpf, Crawford and Bodine (1997) suggest that peer mediation involves the following six steps:

Step 1 Agree to mediate
Introductions
State ground rules

Step 2 Gather points of view
Ask each person what has happened
Ask each person if they want to add anything

Step 3 Focus on interests
Focus on common interests
Determine and summarise shared interests

Step 4 Create win-win options
Brainstorm solutions and ask those involved what could be done to resolve the problem

Step 5 Evaluate options and choose a solution
Ask each person what can be done to resolve the conflict

Step 6 Create an agreement
Write or agree a way forward
Sign or shake hands on the agreement.

If you are interested in setting up a peer mediation system within your class consultation with the Behaviour Support Service or Educational Psychology Service may help you.

Relationships

Year 5

Objective 1: **To recognise the power of discrimination and the impact that it may have on people.**

Suggested activities

The children could be involved in a simulation exercise to give them first hand experience of feeling marginalised and discriminated against. In order to do this the children need to be sorted into two groups. Criteria that may be used by the teacher to split the children into groups include having an 'a' in their name, having blonde hair or being left-handed. At this point it is important that the children are unaware of the criteria for discrimination. For one hour the groups of children should be treated differently, with one group receiving more privileges. After approximately three quarters of the allocated time begin to tell the children the discrimination criteria. For example, 'You can't do this because you've got an 'a' in your name'. Once the exercise has finished it is crucial that the children are debriefed on the purpose of the activity. Sufficient time should be allowed for reflection and discussion, with the emotions evoked during the experience being emphasised.

Many different follow up activities could result from this activity. These include:

- Writing poems about the experience.

- Researching examples of similar types of discrimination in history e.g. the Jews during World War ll, possibly using Anne Frank's Diary as a stimulus.

- Creating abstract pieces of art focusing on the feelings resulting from discrimination.

- Finding, listening to and considering songs that focus on discrimination such as Negro-Spirituals.

- Creating their own songs to reflect feelings associated with discrimination.

Objective 2: **To raise awareness of discrimination within society, focussing on sexism, racism or disability.**

Suggested activities

The children should be given the opportunity to find real life examples of sexual, racial or disability discrimination. To facilitate this TV clips, the internet or newspaper cuttings could be used. Initially the children should be divided into groups to find one example of either sexual, racial or disability discrimination that they then research in detail. This could then be shared with the rest of the class who debate whether or not the example constituted discrimination. A vote could ultimately determine the overall opinion of the class.

The children could then research examples (local and national/international) of schemes designed to tackle racism, disability and sexism. Examples include the Paralympics, 'Kick the racism out of football' and aid schemes to improve the lives of women in third world countries. After researching existing initiatives the children could develop their own ways of tackling discrimination (possibly within their own school) and present these to the rest of the class.

Discussion of the children's personal experiences of sexual, racial or disability discrimination should take place during the secure environment of Circle Time using activities such as:

- Silent statements: 'If you have experienced racial discrimination in the last year swap places.' Those children that do swap places could be asked if they would like to share this incident with the rest of the group.

- Sentence completion: 'The last time I was discriminated against was ... (when I was not allowed to play football with the boys because I am a girl) I have seen discrimination happening when ... (shops do not have ramps as this prevents wheelchair users from entering the shop)'.

Having focused on how and when people are discriminated against, emphasis should now be given to celebrating difference. Children could brainstorm ways in which this could be achieved. For example, one school can link with another school that has a different population, such as boys' or girls' schools, special or mainstream schools and schools with different racial mixes. These schools could then come together and share foods, sports, music, etc.

Objective 3: **Encouragement of equality of opportunity for all.**

Suggested activities
The class could draw up a set of guidelines designed to raise awareness of issues surrounding equal opportunity within their school. These could be displayed in poster form around the school.

Groups of children could act as 'consultants' to other classes in school. Initially they would need to visit the class and through discussion with the teacher and children identify any areas in which some members of the class feel unfairly treated. Following this the group could work together in order to try and resolve the issue relating to inequality of opportunity for the class. This could then be reported back to the class and follow up work carried out if necessary.

Relationships

Year 6

Objective 1: To develop some of the skills involved in successful negotiation.

Suggested activities

Initially the children should be reminded of the conflict resolution work carried out in Year 4 (see p.88). They could then be introduced to negotiation as one way of resolving a conflict successfully (win-win outcome). The children could watch examples of negotiation taken from television programmes and/or films. While watching these clips the children should be encouraged to note the both the skills and the process involved in a negotiation. The notes that the children have taken can then be shared either in small groups or as a whole class. As a result of this discussion the class can make a poster showing the 'steps to successful negotiation'. These should include:

1. State your view

2. Listen to the other person's point of view

3. Identify the goals of both people

4. List possible solutions together

5. Choose the best solution for both of you

6. Evaluate the outcome.

In addition they could also note the personal skills required to negotiate successfully. These should include:

- Listening

- Empathy

- Clear expression

- Assertiveness

- Calm manner

- Ability to problem solve.

The next step is for the children to practise using their negotiation skills in a safe environment. They should use the 'steps to a successful negotiation' posters produced previously to help them. The children could be given cards that outline a conflict situation and use these as the basis for a role play. Following the role play the children should be asked to discuss their feelings during the negotiation process and any difficulties that were encountered while they were negotiating. They can then present these to the class who can consider how such difficulties could be overcome. If necessary these suggestions or strategies could be used to add more detail to the original posters.

Objective 2: **To begin using negotiation within everyday situations.**

Suggested activities

The children could explore situations, both at home and at school, when negotiation would be a useful strategy. These may include falling out over allocation of household tasks at home, falling out with friends at school because they will not let you join in their game or group, what time to return home in the evening or how best to complete a given task.

The children should now have all of the information that they need to make a personal plan outlining where, when and how they plan to use negotiation in their daily lives (Appendix 24, p.124). An example is given below:

Where I plan to use negotiation	When I plan to use negotiation	How I will negotiate	Review: How am I doing?
School	When Fred will not let me join in his game	I will explain why I want to play, listen to what he has to say, help to think of ways that we can play together and then try this out.	This worked and we agreed that I would play with him on a Monday, Wednesday and Friday. We are both happy with this.
Home	When I am asked to lay the table every night and I do not like it.	I will explain to my mum that I do not like laying the table, listen to why she needs me to do it, identify what we both want, think of ways that we can solve this solution and try one of these out.	This worked well. I realised that while mum was cooking the dinner she couldn't set the table as well and mum listened to me. We decided that my brother and I could take it in turns and I will take it in turns to do his drying up. We are all happy with this.

The children should be given opportunities to evaluate these plans and update them if necessary on a regular basis. If they have a problem situation that they are struggling to resolve they may like to raise this during a Circle Time session so that the rest of the class can help them.

References

DfES (2000) *Curriculum Guidance for the Foundation Stage.* London: DfES.

DfES (2003) *Developing Children's Social, Emotional and Behavioural Skills.* London: DfES.

DfES (2004) *Promoting Social, Emotional and Behavioural Skills in Primary Schools.* London: DfES.

DfES (2005) *Excellence and Enjoyment: Social and Emotional Aspects of Learning.* London: DfES.

Durlak, J. (1995) *School Based Intervention Programmes for Children and Adolescents.* London: Sage.

Durlak, J. and Wells, A. (1997) Primary prevention mental health programs for children and adolescents: A meta-analytic review. *American Journal of Community Psychology,* 25 (2): 115–152.

Elias, M., Zins, J., Weissberg, R., Frey, K., Greenberg, M., Haynes, N., Kessler, R., Schwab-Stone, M. and Shriver, T. (1997) *Promoting Social and Emotional Learning.* Virginia: Alexandria ASCD.

Faupel, A., Herrick. and Sharp, P. (1998) *Anger Management: A Practical Guide.* London: David Fulton.

Goleman, D. (1995) *Emotional Intelligence.* London: Bloomsbury.

Greenhalgh, P. (1994) *Emotional Growth and Learning.* London: Routledge.

Mayer, J. and Salovey, P. (1997) What is Emotional Intelligence? In Salovey, P. and Sluyter, D. (eds), *Emotional Development and Emotional Intelligence: Educational Implications.* New York: Basic Books.

Schrumpf, F., Crawford, D. and Bodine, R. (1997) *Peer Mediation: Conflict Resolution in Schools.* Champaign, IL: Research Press.

Stacey, H. and Robinson, P. (1997) *Let's Mediate: A Teachers Guide to Peer Support and Conflict Resolution Skills for All Ages.* London: Sage.

Weare, K. and Gray, G. (2003) *What Works in Developing Children's Emotional and Social Competence and Wellbeing?* London: DfES.

Resources

Websites
www.data.learn.com – The Feelings Game, Facial Expressions
www.bbc.co.uk/cbeebies
www.bandapilot.org.uk – Resources for SEAL

Books

For a full list of books go to www.nelig.com/resources

These are some of our favourites:

Author	Title	Emotions	Publisher
Anderson, H.C.	Emperor's New Clothes	proud, ashamed	Usbourne
Atkinson, E.	Greyfriars Bobby	love, sad	Orion
Carle, E.	The Very Lonely Firefly	lonely	Putnam's
Carle, E.	The Bad Tempered Ladybird	angry	Puffin
Donaldson, J.	The Gruffalo	brave	Macmillan
Frank, A.	The Diary of Anne Frank	brave, scared	Longman
Holm, A.	I Am David	lonely, sad, brave	Mammoth
Hughes, S.	Alfie Gives a Hand	kind, shy, helpful	Red Fox
Hughes, S.	Dogger	sad, kind, happy	Red Fox
Magorian, M.	Goodnight Mister Tom	love, sad, frustrated, proud, kind, scared	Puffin
Mayer, M.	There's a Nightmare in My Cupboard	scared	Puffin
McKee, D.	Not Now, Bernard	frustrated	Red Fox
Munsch, R.	The Paperbag Princess	brave	Scholastic
Murphy, J.	Peace at Last	frustrated	Macmillan
Pfister, M.	Rainbow Fish and the Big Blue Whale	angry, brave, lonely	North South
Pfister, M.	Rainbow Fish to the Rescue	kind, brave	North South
Pfister, M.	Rainbow Fish	kind, sad, proud	North South
Ross, T.	Boy Who Cried Wolf	dishonest, sad	Red Fox
Sendak, M.	Where the Wild Things Are	angry	Red Fox
Varley, S.	Badger's Parting Gifts	sad, love	Picture Lions
Waddell, M.	Owl Babies	scared	Walker
Wilde, O.	The Selfish Giant	mean, kind, unhappy, selfish	Puffin
Wilhelm, H.	I'll Always Love You	love, sad	Tiger Press

Appendices

To contents of the Appendicies are printable from the accompanying CD Rom.

Appendix 1

HAPPY/SAD CARDS

(These could be laminated for use on
more than one occasion)

Appendix 2

FEELINGS CARDS

Appendix 3

FEELINGS CHART: HOW DO I FEEL TODAY

When I arrive in school	After play time	After lunch	Home time

Appendix 4

SITUATION CARDS

The football you are playing with goes through the window	A boy comes up to you and hits you	You're given some work that is too difficult	You are playing a skipping game with a friend
You are blowing out the candles on your birthday cake	Two cars crash outside school	Your favourite pet dog dies	Your football team loses a match
You are at the airport waiting to go on holiday	You get a new pair of shoes	You have a nightmare in the night	Your friend comes to your house for tea
Someone in your class breaks your favourite toy	Your grandparents arrive to stay for a week	You have to go to the supermarket with your mum	You are going on a school trip
Your mum takes you swimming	You get told off by your teacher	You fall over and cut your knee	Your friend tells you a joke
A girl in your class is rude about your family	Your friend falls in a puddle but does not hurt themselves	You get chased by a dog in the park	You win a prize
It rains when you are supposed to be going for a picnic in the park	You go on a roller coaster at the fair	You have no-one to play with at playtime	You watch your favourite TV programme
You are asked to read a story out loud in assembly	You lose your pocket money	You start at a new school where you do not know anyone	Your gran is very ill
Your mum and dad split up	Your teacher leaves your school	You are asked to play the recorder in the school concert	Your mum is going to buy you a dog

Appendix 5

FEELING CARDS

Happy	Sad	Scared	Excited
Angry	Frustrated	Upset	Shy
Lonely	Proud	Pleased	Jealous
Embarrassed	Content	Afraid	Grief
Ashamed	Nervous	Anxious	Bored
Relaxed	Miserable	Excited	Curious
Determined	Impatient	Ecstatic	Brave
Insecure	Relieved	Shocked	Bold
Delighted	Frightened	Optimistic	Shy
Disappointed	Annoyed	Accepted	Violent
Grieving	Worried	Elated	Peaceful
Intimidated	Hopeful	Distracted	Envious
Exhilarated	Overwhelmed	Confident	Guilty
Infuriated	Affectionate	Fearful	Helpless

Appendix 6

FEELINGS DIARY (YEAR 2)

How do I feel?	Why do I feel like this?	Is it OK to feel like this?

Appendix 7

FEELINGS DIARY (YEAR 3)

How do I feel?	Why do I feel like this?	Is it OK to feel like this?	Is it helpful to feel like this?

Appendix 8

FEELINGS DIARY (YEAR 4)

Date	Feeling	Trigger to my feeling	Cue changes in my body

Appendix 9

ACTION CARDS

You are sent off in a game of football for arguing with the referee	You win a swimming race	You are invited to a birthday party	You get 1/10 on a spelling test
You accidentally break a cup at home	You choose a new coat	You are breaking up from school for the summer holiday	You win a drawing competition
You sleep over at your friend's house	You help your mum cook your favourite dinner	You lose your favourite toy/game	You are allowed to go to the shop by yourself
You shout at your best friend because they ignore you	You are told off by your teacher for copying	You drop a bottle of tomato sauce in the supermarket	You nearly get run over crossing the road
You fall off your bike	You argue with your brother/sister	You are not allowed to watch your favourite TV programme	You are sent to your bedroom
You do not want to go to school	You go out to play with your friends	You take your new puppy for a walk	You move house
You read your story to the class because it is good	You find your school work very difficult	Your brother messes up your bedroom	You go on a roller coaster ride at the fair
You go to the library to choose a book	You buy some chocolates for your mum	You don't want to do your homework	You offer to play with someone new in your class
You help your teacher tidy the classroom at lunchtime	You find your homework too difficult	You have to start wearing glasses	You don't understand what you have been asked to do

Appendix 10

THOUGHT CARDS

My mum will shout at me	I was only getting my ball out of the road	It will be exciting tonight	I'm so lucky
I can't wait until it is over	I think my dad trusts me	All of my practice made me good at this	My teacher must think that I am clever
I don't like places where there are lots of people and noise	I like living near to my friends	They do not like me anymore	I enjoy helping my mum
They never listen to me	Now everyone will think that I am stupid	I like it when I am allowed to choose	I need to ask for help
I know what it is like to feel lonely	They will not pick me next time because we lost the match	Why does he always annoy me?	I don't care
I will miss my friends	I don't like spelling tests	It's not fair	I knew I did badly because I did not practice
This might cheer her up	The shopkeeper will be angry with me	My mum will be pleased with me	At least I do not have to go out to play
What am I going to do without it?	I will get teased by my friends	I don't know what it will be like	I can't do this
What is this all about?	This is boring	I was not thinking about what I was doing	I have got better things to do

Appendix 11a

EMOTIONAL TRANSITIONS

How do you feel now?	How you might feel next
Angry	Guilty
Scared	Relieved
Upset	Sad
Upset	Frustrated
Bored	Disappointed
Excited	
Lonely	
Happy	
Jealous	
Nervous	
Embarrassed	
Proud	

Appendix 11b

EMOTIONAL TRANSITIONS

How do you feel now?	How you might feel next

Appendix 12a

HOW DO THEY FEEL
AND
HOW CAN YOU HELP?

Sarah has just fallen out with her friend Jane. Jane had been saying nasty things about Sarah and her family to other people in their class and Sarah has found out. Sarah had trusted Jane and had talked to her about the arguments that her mum and dad were having at home.

How does Sarah feel and how could you help?

Appendix 12b

HOW DO THEY FEEL AND HOW CAN YOU HELP?

Phillip has arranged to meet his friend John at the cinema. John arrives 15 minutes late and then says that he does not want to see the film that they had decided to watch.

How does Phillip feel and what would be the best way of dealing with this situation?

Appendix 13

SIMULTANEOUS FEELINGS
PROMPT CARDS FOR ROLE PLAYS

Situation/Event	Simultaneous Feelings
Going to your friend's birthday party	Excited and jealous
Starting at a new school	Lonely and nervous
Your pet goldfish dies	Upset and disappointed
You score the winning goal in a football match	Proud and happy
You are watching your favourite TV programme	Relaxed and happy
You are about to go on a new fast rollercoaster	Anxious and excited
Singing in front of a lot of people	Embarrassed and nervous
You cannot find the T-shirt that you are looking for	Frustrated and annoyed
You hear a big bang in the night	Shocked and scared
You cannot think of a game to play	Bored and frustrated
It is Tuesday morning and you are really looking forward to the weekend	Impatient and excited
A spelling test that you have practised very hard for	Determined and relaxed
You accidentally break your friend's ruler	Guilty and worried

Appendix 14a

EMOTION CARDS

Happy	Sad	Afraid	Angry
Excited	Bored	Relaxed	Worried
Upset	Hurt	Tired	Shy

Appendix 14b

EMOTION CARDS

Appendix 15a

ACTION CARDS

Laughing	Hitting	Crying
Running away	Jumping up and down	Smiling
Hiding	Kicking	Screaming
Clapping your hands	Sitting quietly	Yawning

Appendix 15b

ACTION CARDS

Appendix 16

ROLE PLAY SCENARIOS

Fred is feeling bored in class	**Jenny sees a spider in the room and is scared**
Rachel spills paint on her skirt and is worried	**Gary can't do his work and is feeling annoyed**
Paul is upset because he was hit by Stephen at playtime	**Emily is sad because the teacher shouted at her**
Sarah is lonely at playtime	**Richard is happy because it is his birthday**
Michael is bored because he has nothing to do	**Hasan is angry because he is not allowed to go outside at playtime**
Elizabeth is nervous because she does not want to read her work in assembly	**Ayesha is excited because she has got a new baby sister**

Appendix 17

WHAT IS ACCEPTABLE AND WHAT IS UNACCEPTABLE?

Screaming	Laughing	Walking away
Smiling	Hitting	Swearing
Crying	Singing	Kicking
Shouting	Singing	Swearing
Jumping up and down	Calling others' names	Biting others
Sucking your thumb	Clapping your hands	Biting your nails
Throwing things	Pinching	Asking questions
Lying	Asking someone to stop	Apologising
Fiddling with something nearby	Closing your eyes	Stamping your feet

Appendix 18

MANAGING MY EMOTIONS (1)

Date	Trigger	Emotion	Strategy	Improvement

MANAGING MY EMOTIONS (2)

Trigger	Emotion(s)	Thought	Action

Appendix 20

AMBIGUOUS SCENARIOS/PICTURES

Someone knocks your arm when you are winning in class

Your teacher does not answer you when you ask a question

Your friend ignores you as you walk past

Someone pushes you in the playground

Someone takes your best pen off your desk

Your coat is on the floor in the cloakroom at home-time

Appendix 21

ROLE PLAY SCENARIOS

Cameron falls out with Billy because Billy does not share his sweets	Tina falls out with Hayley because she is not invited to join in Hayley's game
Michelle and Gemma fall out because Gemma hit Michelle in a game	Lee falls out with Abdul because Abdul blames Lee for something he has not done
Simon falls out with Rachel because he hears Rachel calling him names	Sharon and Justine fall out because Sharon will not share her skipping rope
Taylor and Jason fall out because Jason will not let Taylor play in his football team at playtime	Andrea falls out with Kate because Kate accidentally rips Andrea's work
Sarah falls out with her brother Max because he will not let her watch her favourite programme	Ismail falls out with Craig because when Craig threw a ball it accidentally hit Ismail on the head
Mark and Andrew fall out because Mark shouts at Andrew at playtime	James and Antony fall out when Antony will not help James with his work
Sue and Rebecca fall out after an argument about what Sue did at the weekend	Jodie falls out with Kim because Kim tells lies about something

Appendix 22

PERSONAL PROFILES

Things that I'm good at	Things I need help with

Appendix 23

WAYS OF DEALING WITH CONFLICT

Walking away	Talking/negotiating away	Hit someone and walk
Ask an adult for help	Shout at someone	Fight
Get your friends to gang up on someone	Offer suggestions of things to do next	Ignore someone
Compromise	Argue	Swear at someone
Apologise have to say	Listen to what people	Laughing/telling a joke
Punch a wall	Kick someone	Crying
Ask a friend for help	Always thinking you are right and others are wrong	Calling someone names

Appendix 24

NEGOTIATION

Where I plan to use negotiation	When I plan to use negotiation	How I will negotiate	Review: How am I doing?